D1055336

THOMAS JEFFERSON

THOMAS JEFFERSON

America's Philosopher-King

MAX LERNER

Edited and with
an introduction
by Robert Schmuhl

TRANSACTION PUBLISHERS
New Brunswick (U.S.A.) and London (U.K.)

Library of Congress Catalog Number: 96-3232
ISBN: 1-56000-262-X
Printed in the United States of America

Library of Congress Cataloging-in-Publication Data

Lerner, Max, 1902–
    Thomas Jefferson : America's philosopher-king / Max Lerner ; edited and with an introduction by Robert Schmuhl.
        p. cm.
    Includes bibliographical references and index.
    ISBN 1-56000-262-X (alk. paper)
    1. Jefferson, Thomas, 1743–1826. 2. Presidents—United States—Biography. I. Schmuhl, Robert. II. Title.
E332.2.L47   1996
973.4'6'092—dc20   96-3232
[B]   CIP

Contents

Preface and Acknowledgments

Max Lerner first began work on a book about Thomas Jefferson not long after the publication of his monumental study, *America as a Civilization,* in 1957. Lerner originally envisioned a volume with a lengthy interpretive essay, a selection of Jefferson's writings, and several statements of editorial commentary about the different kinds of prose chosen for inclusion. Once published, the book would take its place (Lerner thought) next to an earlier one he similarly constructed, *The Mind and Faith of Justice Holmes,* which appeared in 1943 in the first of several editions.

Throughout the 1960s and into the 1970s, Lerner kept returning to the Jefferson project. Unfortunately, other writing assignments, academic responsibilities, and lecture dates in this country and abroad made it difficult to complete a sprawling book with several parts. However, in diary jottings and other notes discovered after his death in 1992, Lerner's continuing interest in finishing his volume on Jefferson becomes clear.

Entries and letters suggest different titles. Initially, in 1959, "Jefferson: A Profile in History," appeals to him. Then, in 1967, the subtitle "The Life and Thought of Thomas Jefferson" follows a number of possible main titles: "Revolutionary and Humanist," "Revolutionary Giant," "Radical Humanist," and "Complete American, Complete Man." By 1970 Lerner was calling the book "America's Philosopher-King: The Mind and Faith of Thomas Jefferson." Later in the 1970s and until his death, Lerner gave up the idea of publishing the selections from Jefferson's writing, yet he kept seeing the possibility of what he called a "biographical-interpretive book." The relatively brief volume, "Thomas Jefferson: America's Philosopher-King," would introduce a thinker and public figure of enduring pertinence to a general reader.

A few weeks before he died, Lerner asked me to work on what he had completed to try to get the manuscript into shape for publication. At the time, many of the pages were in finished typescript form. Others, though, included changes or suggestions of references requiring incorporation into the work as a whole. All the editing that has been done reflects Lerner's intentions as faithfully as they could be rendered.

Irving Louis Horowitz, Editorial Chairman and President Emeritus of Transaction Publishers, encouraged the completion of this book and deserves more than a word of grateful thanks. Since 1989, Professor Horowitz, with characteristic wisdom and an abiding concern for keeping valuable ideas alive, has overseen Transaction's publication of five new editions of books by Max Lerner—*It Is Later Than You Think* (1989), *The Mind and Faith of Justice Holmes* (1989), *Ideas Are Weapons* (1991), *Ideas for the Ice Age* (1992), and *Tocqueville and American Civilization* (1994)—each with new material, as well as two never-before-published volumes—*Magisterial Imagination: Six Masters of the Human Sciences* (1994) and this book.

Edna Albers Lerner is unfailingly kind in offering the help and support of the Lerner family. I am also grateful for the continuing advice and counsel of Michael and Stephen Lerner. And Evelyn Irsay, Max Lerner's assistant for several years, is always there to offer help.

The University of Notre Dame's Institute for Scholarship in the Liberal Arts, directed so ably by Associate Dean Jennifer Warlick, provided an appreciated (and much-needed) travel grant that allowed me to work on the manuscript while it was among the Lerner papers in California. Nancy Kegler, chief assistant in the Department of American Studies at Notre Dame, skillfully ushered yet another book project to completion. And Thomas J. Stritch, professor emeritus of American Studies at Notre Dame, read an early draft of the introduction and proposed several useful suggestions for improving it.

Finally, Judith Roberts Schmuhl and Michael Robert Schmuhl realize that doing books of one kind or another often require time that otherwise might be spent happily with them. They respect this and other obsessions, and I remain more than grateful to them.

—R.S.

Introduction

Max Lerner was attracted to Thomas Jefferson as to no other American president. He saw in Jefferson reflections of what he himself most rootedly believed. For Jefferson, above all, was a figure of the Enlightenment, with its dedication to rationalism, liberalism, and humanitarianism. Like Jefferson, Lerner thought freedom of inquiry a *sine qua non* of human existence. Yet, both Jefferson and Lerner recognized that a free-roaming life of the mind goes just so far, and that intellectual pursuits often have greater, more lasting consequences when they are directed outwardly, to the benefit of others in a wider community.

To Lerner, Jefferson came closest in the American context to Plato's suggestion in the *Republic* of a "philosopher-king." Ironically, however, Jefferson was a devoted democrat and disliked any hints of monarchic traits or trappings in the new American republic. Lerner, too, was an unwavering champion of democracy and merit, who also favored a simplicity of manners. But Plato's concept of a thinker *and* leader seemed appropriate to Lerner in stressing Jefferson's virtues and implying his unique place in United States history.

Moreover, in lectures and essays, Lerner was fond of repeating two quotations: Henri Bergson's charge to a gathering of philosophers, "Act as men of thought, think as men of action," and a sentence from a speech by Oliver Wendell Holmes, Jr., "As life is action and passion, it is required of a man that he should share the passion and action of his time at peril of being judged not to have lived."[1] In Jefferson, Lerner saw the embodiment of both statements. Thought, action, and passion intertwined in a succession of historic deeds that forever changed the colonies and the new nation.

Lerner studied and assessed many presidents during more than six decades as an author, journalist, and professor, yet Jefferson received the most sustained attention. A widely syndicated columnist for almost half-a-century, Lerner personally knew and interviewed several presidents. However, he kept retreating to the past and returning to Jefferson

1

for developed analysis and commentary. Identification with particular aspects of the Virginian's life and thought was certainly one reason for this focus. Another, and undoubtedly more compelling one, was the complexity, indeed ambiguity, of Jefferson that proved irresistible to the Russian-born writer, who devoted so much of his career to explaining America's characteristics and contradictions to his adopted country and to the world.

Besides possessing specific traits Lerner admired, Jefferson was a generalist and man of letters for whom little, if anything, was foreign. Despite the extraordinary emphasis on academic specialization during the twentieth century, Lerner always considered himself a generalist. He sought connections and context. Devotion to disciplinary rigor had its place, especially in plumbing the depths of a subject. Yet trying to see the wholeness of life, how different aspects relate to each other in a pattern with meaning and consequence, was Lerner's abiding interest. His restless mind wandered widely, and none of what he called "the human sciences" was foreign to him.[2] In book after book, article after article, he discovered imaginative interrelationships among subjects, and he presented these insights in vivid, arresting prose. Lerner himself was very much a man of letters, the master of several different literary forms— short and long essays, book-length studies, memoirs, even poetry.

Jefferson's efforts to combine political philosophy with the practice of politics (seeking office and actually governing) attracted Lerner, who helped write the statement articulating the Four Freedoms for Franklin D. Roosevelt's administration, and later even toyed with the possibility of running for the United States Senate from New York during the 1960s. American democracy, complete with its possibilities and problems, absorbed both men—but never limited them. Their visions were wider and more encompassing. As democracy replaced totalitarian communism in Eastern Europe and elsewhere during the late 1980s and early 1990s, Lerner took pleasure in noting that Jefferson's words and ideals helped direct movements abroad to gain freedom and citizen participation.

Of equal, if not greater concern was the life of the mind, with each in his way recognizing the importance of education to a free society. Jefferson, of course, wrote at length on the subject and subsequently founded the University of Virginia. Being "Father of the University of Virginia" as well as "Author of the Declaration of American Independence [and] of the Statute of Virginia for religious freedom" were

Jefferson's proudest accomplishments and what he directed to be chiseled on his tombstone. Serving two terms as president didn't merit inclusion. Lerner spent much of his life teaching—at Sarah Lawrence, Williams, Harvard, Brandeis, Notre Dame, and United States International University—and he repeatedly advanced proposals to improve the American educational system. Most notably, he outlined and presented his reflections on what he termed "the teaching-learning process" in two books: *Education and a Radical Humanism* (1962) and *Values in Education: Notes Toward a Values Philosophy* (1976).

Showing similarities or pointing out parallels is by no means an attempt at equating these two men; far from it. They were distinctly different with distinctly different achievements. However, their shared interests and life purposes provide some hints as to why Jefferson had such abiding, almost haunting, appeal for Lerner. In many respects, Jefferson was the exemplar—the intellectual man of action, blessed with literary skill and a fervent commitment to democracy and America. Jefferson's distinctions in several realms were all the more remarkable to Lerner because they worked together, creating wholeness in a fully integrated person, who possessed many connected traits and kept pursuing a larger objective. In public office and private life, Jefferson followed the lodestar of freedom. The path took numerous directions, but there was always a point of convergence. Lerner recognized the merits of Jefferson's continuing exploration and saw a uniqueness in him worth extended probing.

Prior to beginning his work on Jefferson, Lerner completed similar studies of Oliver Wendell Holmes, Jr. and Alexis de Tocqueville. In both of the earlier instances, Lerner prepared lengthy biographical and critical essays to precede specific written works—in Holmes's case an extensive collection of his articles, speeches, legal opinions, and letters, and with Tocqueville, a new edition of *Democracy in America*.[3] Tackling Jefferson started a new phase in Lerner's career, a period encompassing the three decades before his death, when the presidency and individual presidents received considerably more focused attention than before. He had written extensively about the Supreme Court during the 1930s and early 1940s, and *America as a Civilization* occupied much of his time in the decade after the Second World War.

However, from 1960 until his death in 1992, there was more deliberate concentration on the White House and on those who occupied the nation's highest elective office. To be sure, presidential matters, both governing and campaigning, had been recurring subjects for Lerner to analyze over the years, especially for the newspaper column he began writing in 1943. However, in dealing with Jefferson, you see the start of sustained inquiry, including several comprehensive essays, university classes, and public lectures exclusively devoted to the presidency and leadership, and outlines for several unfinished books surveying individual presidents within the forces and circumstances of their times.

In considering Jefferson, Lerner combines biographical information, historical background, and analytical commentary. The result is a primer about Jefferson that not only describes his accomplishments, but discusses his problems and failures. Respectful admiration, even a certain affinity for his subject, did not sway Lerner from providing a balanced, at times robustly critical assessment. For example, chapter 6 ("Jefferson in Power") and chapter 7 ("Jefferson in Trouble") illustrate this approach. One chapter vigorously chronicles the successes of Jefferson's first years as president, while the other pointedly enumerates the shortcomings of the second term. Although always a writer with strong personal opinions and convictions, Lerner prized fairness and steady judgment in his analysis. He also sought whenever possible to relate the past to the present, and one sees him making such connections throughout his treatment of Jefferson.

Busy with his regular column, magazine assignments, teaching, public lectures, and frequent trips abroad, Lerner had some difficulty completing book projects after the publication of *America as a Civilization* in 1957 and *The Age of Overkill* in 1962. Off and on, he spent well over a decade doing the research and writing for his study of Jefferson. Several drafts exist, all with handwritten additions and emendations. Lerner also selected and arranged hundreds of pages of Jefferson's writings. These works were intended to show literary mastery and substantive breadth, besides being early Republic documents with continuing resonance.

Lerner set aside what he had completed of the Jefferson manuscript in the early 1970s. This means, among other things, that Lerner's commentary in this book predates studies emphasizing Jefferson's private life, such as Fawn M. Brodie's pathbreakingly controversial *Thomas Jefferson: An Intimate History,* which appeared in 1974. However, what Brodie and others wrote intrigued Lerner, and he dealt with their findings and conclusions in an essay published in 1977. In one section of the lengthy essay, he notes:

> Jefferson's relationships with women have become the thorniest problem for his biographers. He had a strong commitment to his wife, Martha, who died when he was still a young man of 39, and whose death shook him. But the assumption of most who have written about him, that this great and good man must have forsworn sexuality for the rest of his life, doesn't necessarily follow. The efforts to sanctify him, as if he were a spinsterish clergyman figure, do justice neither to his intense, passionate nature nor to his basic character as a complex, many-sided, total person.

> The storm has raged around the question of Jefferson's relationship to two women— Maria Cosway, American wife of a dandified British miniature painter, who lived in London and visited in Paris while Jefferson was Minister; and Sally Hemings, a slave girl at Jefferson's Monticello home, who was also an illegitimate half sister to Jefferson's wife. Jefferson and Maria Cosway unquestionably had a romantic love affair, as evidenced by Jefferson's famous long letter, "Dialogue between My Head and My Heart," which he wrote out of his heartbreak when Maria had to leave Paris for London. They exchanged 25 more letters, described by Fawn Brodie as "the most remarkable collection of love letters in the history of the American presidency." Mrs. Brodie's detailed and scholarly psychohistory, *Thomas Jefferson: An Intimate History*, argues persuasively that their relationship was sexual as well as romantic, but that neither of the lovers dared make the break into a marriage which both must have thought of.

> The scholarly controversy over Sally Hemings has been even stormier, with Jefferson's traditional biographers dismissing as libel the contention that she was Jefferson's mistress from the days of his Paris household and bore him four children, and with Fawn Brodie marshaling her artillery of evidence to assert it was true. The reader who wants to decide for himself must go to Dumas Malone's masterly...volumes on Jefferson's life...and to Mrs. Brodie's massive and lively 800-page book. It is interesting that recent black writers, who uniformly attack Jefferson for having continued to own slaves despite his passionate defense of human freedom, are inclined to accept the Sally Hemings story as part of the facts of life about Virginia's plantation morals.

> My own guess is that they and Fawn Brodie have the better of the controversy. In his relationships with women, Jefferson seems to have been attracted to the difficult and the forbidden. He was trapped in an age, a class, and a society where miscegenation was practiced but severely punished when made public. He couldn't have escaped a feeling of guilt about this relationship, as suggested by his long history of migraine headaches. This doesn't negate my view of him as a whole man, although a complex and guilt-ridden one. Yeats put it well: "Nothing can be sole or whole/That has not been rent."[4]

The word "complex" appears twice in the quotation above. Lerner returns to this fact of Jefferson's life near the end of the essay: "The legend that crystallized after his death made him out to have been bigger than life, so complex that his name and writings were invoked for every cause—conservative, liberal, and radical angles of vision, weak and strong presidencies. Everyone saw him through the prism of his own political coloration. But of one fact there could be no doubt—the many-sidedness of his devouring mind."

Both in this essay and throughout the longer study on which it is based, Jefferson's magisterial complexity is the principal vein Lerner works in interpreting a poly-dimensional figure. In clear, accessible prose, he bores to the essential elements of Jefferson's thinking and action, words and deeds. Lerner's often noted abilities to synthesize and to untangle knotty realities for a general reading audience give this book as much relevance now as when it was written.

In its way, *Thomas Jefferson: America's Philosopher-King* contributes to the renewed, indeed flourishing, interest in Jefferson that has been so evident in recent years. The publication of Brodie's book, Garry Wills's *Inventing America: Jefferson's Declaration of Independence* in 1978, and the sixth volume of Dumas Malone's *Thomas Jefferson and His Times* in 1981 helped stimulate further scholarly work, including Willard Sterne Randall's muscular reinterpretation, *Thomas Jefferson: A Life* (1993). The cover article in the November, 1992 issue of *The Atlantic Monthly* was Douglas L. Wilson's "Thomas Jefferson and the Character Issue," which examines many of the problems of trying to deal with the past by using "present-day preoccupations."

Since the 1970s, as political figures have declined in esteem and the media have been more inclined to probe previously private facets of a person's life, historians, biographers, and others have shown greater interest in revealing personal details about prominent figures who are dead. Jefferson, in particular, has received such treatment, and it has taken several forms—from serious scholarly scrutiny to works of popular entertainment. In 1993, two much-noted novels—Steve Erickson's *Arc d'X* and Max Byrd's *Jefferson*—used Jefferson's life out of the public's view as the bases for fictional narratives. Two years later, the movie *Jefferson in Paris* caused a stir, with historians and critics debating whether indecent liberties were taken with the truth in rendering Jefferson's years abroad and his relationship with Sally Hemings. Interestingly, at almost the same time *Jefferson in Paris* was receiving attention in 1995, the newly installed Speaker of the House of Representatives, Newt Gingrich, inaugurated a computer system, called "Thomas," allowing the public ready access to information about Congress. The Jeffersonian ideal of an informed citizenry was technologically more possible, and the father of the original thought received credit, albeit in cyberspace.

Two centuries after he helped create America, Thomas Jefferson remains a figure of enduring fascination within academic quarters and throughout the public at large. What Max Lerner writes in the pages that follow help explain and clarify not only this unending fascination, but the timeless relevance of the nation's devoutly democratic yet singularly authentic "philosopher-king."

Notes

1. Max Lerner's second collection of newspaper columns was called *Actions and Passions: Notes on the Multiple Revolution of Our Time* (New York: Simon and Schuster, 1949).
2. For a discussion of Lerner as generalist, see the introduction to *Magisterial Imagination: Six Masters of the Human Sciences*, ed. Robert Schmuhl (New Brunswick, N.J.: Transaction Publishers, 1994), x–xi, and Max Lerner, *The Unfinished Country: A Book of American Symbols* (New York: Simon and Schuster, 1959), xvi.
3. See Max Lerner, *The Mind and Faith of Justice Holmes: His Speeches, Essays, Letters and Judicial Opinions* (Boston: Little, Brown, 1943), which was republished with a new afterword essay by Lerner (New Brunswick, N.J.: Transaction Publishers, 1989) and Max Lerner, *Tocqueville and American Civilization* (New York: Harper Colophon Books, 1969), which was reissued, with an introduction by Robert Schmuhl (New Brunswick, N.J.: Transaction Publishers, 1994). Lerner's study of Tocqueville was originally published as the introduction to a new edition of *Democracy in America*, translated by George Lawrence and edited by J. P. Mayer and Max Lerner (New York: Harper and Row, 1966). The studies of both Holmes and Tocqueville can also be found in Max Lerner, *Magisterial Imagination: Six Masters of the Human Sciences*, ed. Robert Schmuhl (New Brunswick, N.J.: Transaction Publishers, 1994).
4. Max Lerner, "The Real Mr. America," *Quest* (January 1977): 25–26.

Chronology of Thomas Jefferson

1743	April 13	Born, Shadwell, Albemarle County, Virginia
1757	August 17	Death of father, Peter Jefferson
1760	March to April 1762	Attended College of William and Mary
1762	April	Entered law office of George Wythe at Williamsburg
1766	May	Traveled to Philadelphia and New York
1767		Admitted to the bar
1769	March	Elected to Virginia House of Burgesses
1772	January 1	Married Martha Wayles Skelton
1772	September 27	Birth of daughter, Martha
1773	October	Appointed surveyor of Albemarle County
1774	April 3	Birth of second daughter, Jane Randolph
1774	August	Published *A Summary View of the Rights of British America*
1775	March	Elected deputy delegate to Continental Congress
1775	June 21 to July 31	Attended Continental Congress at Philadelphia
1775	September	Death of daughter, Jane Randolph
1775	October 2 to December 28	Attended Continental Congress at Philadelphia
1776	June 11	Appointed to committee to draft the Declaration of Independence
1776	June 28	Submitted draft of Declaration
1776	October 11 to December 14	Attended Virginia Assembly at Williamsburg
1776	November 5	Appointed to committee to revise Virginia laws
1777	May 28	Birth of son
1777	June 14	Death of son
1778	August 1	Birth of third daughter, Mary (or Maria)
1779	June 1	Elected Governor of Virginia
1780	June 1	Re-elected Governor of Virginia
1780	November 30	Birth of fourth daughter, Lucy Elizabeth (1st)
1781	April 15	Death of daughter, Lucy Elizabeth (1st)
1781	June 1	Resigned as Governor

1781	June 14	Appointed Peace Commissioner to Europe by Continental Congress
1781	June 30	Declined appointment
1781	November 30	Elected delegate to Congress
1782	May 8	Birth of fifth daughter, Lucy Elizabeth (2nd)
1782	September 6	Death of Mrs. Jefferson
1783	June 6	Elected delegate to Congress
1784	March 12	Elected chairman of Congress
1784	May 7	Appointed Minister to France
1784	August 6	Arrived in Paris
1784	c. October 13	Death of daughter, Lucy Elizabeth (2nd)
1787	September–December	Endorsed Constitution of the United States but urged adding Bill of Rights
1787	December	Published *Notes on the State of Virginia* in England, following earlier private publication
1789	September 25	Nominated to be Secretary of State
1789	September 26	Left Paris
1790	March 22	Became Secretary of State
1793	December 31	Resigned as Secretary of State
1796	November	Elected Vice President of the United States
1797	January	Elected President, American Philosophical Society
1797	March 4	Sworn in as Vice President
1798	October	Drafted Kentucky Resolutions
1800	January 18	Began planning University of Virginia
1800	May	Nominated candidate for President
1801	February 17	Elected President
1801	March 4	Inaugurated as President
1804	April 17	Death of daughter, Mary (Maria) Jefferson Eppes
1804	November	Re-elected President
1805	March 4	Inaugurated as President for second term
1809	March 4	Retired from Presidency
1812	January	Renewal of friendship with John Adams
1826	June 25	Wrote his last letter
1826	July 4	Died at Monticello

1

The Making of a Revolutionary, 1743–1784

In those days in Virginia, as in England, leadership was likely to come from an elite of birth. Virginia government was government by gentry; Thomas Jefferson's father, Peter Jefferson, although a farmer with little education, belonged to the substantial plantation gentry, married a Randolph, became a land surveyor and land speculator, and was drawn into the circles of larger wealth and higher social standing. The eldest son and most talented child in a family of eight children, Thomas was born on 13 April 1743, at Shadwell in what is now Albemarle County, in the Piedmont area of Virginia. For several years, as a very young child, he lived farther east at Tuckahoe, where his father ran a plantation entrusted to him by his Randolph kin. Jefferson's earliest memory was of being transported regally, at the age of three, sitting on a pillow held by a slave on horseback, on the family journey from Shadwell to their temporary home. Later the boy grew up at Shadwell, largely surrounded by womenfolk, but with a strapping vigorous father who had learned the surveyor's craft and who brought into his son's life the eye-opening sense of rough travel and adventure on the western Virginia frontier, which he explored on horse, to spy out new rich soil and survey it and perhaps acquire it by patent from the Governor's Council.

That was how Peter Jefferson himself built up his own landed estate. He became a vestryman, church warden, and a member of the House of Burgesses, and as a self-made and self-taught man he was a sturdy member of the rising gentry of the Virginia middle country. Thomas Jefferson, as his son, stood thus between the Tidewater and the frontier, at the convergence of the aristocratic and democratic impulses in Virginia. One of the remarkable facts about his later development was that he was to remain part of his aristocratic environment, fully at ease in it, yet also transcending it as the militant champion of a populist democracy.

11

At fourteen, on his father's death, Thomas as the eldest son became the head of the family. His inheritance was 2,700 acres of land and a number of slaves, a cherry tree desk, a bookcase with forty volumes, some mathematical and surveying instruments, and the ease of living and the social standing of the Randolph and Jefferson names; but it was also a feeling for his natural environment, a respect for books, a sense of a lucid and ordered life, with the draughtsmanship cleanly done and the account books well kept. The boy probably saw little of his father, who was often away on long exploring and surveying journeys, and from the age of nine to fourteen Tom boarded with a clergyman teacher. Yet, he seems to have identified strikingly with a father who taught him to ride and shoot, took him hunting, and talked to him of the importance of books, who clearly owed nothing to anyone but was his own self-reliant master, with a self that an impressionable, growing boy could use as a model to grow by. To have such a father torn away when you were four-teen was not an easy thing to get over. Possibly it was because his de-pendency needs were unfulfilled that young Jefferson attached himself to several older men as he came of age, and most of his later life acted the father role to a number of younger men.

He got more than a casual, back-country education. For five years before his father's death he studied Latin, Greek, and a little French with a Scottish clergyman, William Douglas, thus getting a "classical education," that rarity in a state that was then almost without formal secondary schools except for a few private "academies." Jefferson got more of his real education from Rev. James Maury, the first of a succes-sion of men who helped shape his character and mind after his father's death. Maury ran a little school on his plantation for a handful of the neighborhood youth, and young Jefferson boarded with him for several years until he was ready for college. They were his early shaping years intellectually, from fourteen to seventeen, and while Maury was a rigid churchman and half a Tory, his mind—with its classical scholarship, its feeling for language and style, its knowledge of literature and of "natu-ral philosophy," the science of the day—left an impress.

What else left an impress on the boy in those years we can only con-jecture: the sweep of the Virginia landscape, with its tobacco fields and its still untamed areas, with the rugged beauty of hill and river and for-est, which was to give meaning to the idea of Nature in Jefferson's thought; the doubtless well-thumbed books in the library his father left him, including some Whig versions of English history, Baron George Anson's *Voyage Round the World in the Years 1740–1744*, volumes of state trials and Virginia laws, and the accepted works of Shakespeare, Swift, Pope, and Addison; a sense of classical history and civilization that came with the study of the classical languages, and perhaps the image of the hero-patriots of antiquity. There was also a hero-patriot in contemporary England, where the dramatic and contagious figure of William Pitt fought a relentless political war against Robert Walpole and the Hanoverian dynasty and, while establishing England's *imperium* from Passy to the plains of Abraham, upheld brilliantly in Whig fashion the rights of freeborn Englishmen against absolute power. One can only guess at what it meant to young Jefferson, at seventeen, to have such models as the Virginia country gentlemen, the patriots of antiquity, and the British Whigs, who showed how politics can be conducted in the grand libertarian style.

Jefferson was not quite seventeen when he entered as a student at the College of William and Mary at Williamsburg—a lanky, freckled, hazel-eyed, reddish-haired youth, with large hands and feet, shy manners, more than a hint of a precocious mind, and earnest habits of reading and application. He was bored to death in the backwater of Shadwell and eager for the larger life that Williamsburg promised as a college and a colonial capital. While many Virginia families preferred an education in England over one in the colonies, young Jefferson was happy at the chance (as he put it in a letter to his guardian) to continue his classics, study mathematics, make friends, and cut down on the expenses of entertainment at Shadwell. The mélange of benefits described in the letter gives us a glimpse of the awkward, shrewd, and hungry mind of the young man who had been thrown on his own resources so early, and had an intellect to shape and a life to make.

The College of William and Mary, where Jefferson was enrolled as a student for two years and a month, had been intended at its founding, in 1693, as a training ground for Anglican clergymen and public servants. With a faculty largely of churchmen it was controlled rather tightly by the Crown, and the British thought it important enough to set aside the colonial tobacco tax as its source of subsidy. By today's standards it was not much of a college, with less than a hundred students, a tiny, quarrel-ridden faculty, only a few courses, and scarcely any equipment for science, a constant guerrilla war over salaries and taxes, and with a

President who drank because of his crises and was dismissed because he drank. Yet for Jefferson it proved to have three essentials for a great education: fellow students who together comprised the recognized blood and ability of Virginia; a teacher of stature who also brought Jefferson into the close circle of his friends; and Williamsburg itself as a political community, to serve as a smith for the forging of a political mind.

Each of these three elements deserves an added note. The college was a cradle of talent, very much as Oxford and Cambridge were, but the landowner strain was, if anything, less diluted than in England with the sons of merchants and parsons. Jefferson's talent for friendship gave him a recognized place among the sons of the Virginia planter elite—the Pages, Carrs, Walkers, Garrisons, Randolphs, Amblers, Skeltons, Moores, Tylers, and Eppeses. He was not plagued by the class feeling that one found in the later English universities, nor the status insecurities of the later American ones. He could devote himself, even in a provincial Virginia village, to the languages, mathematics, natural history, music, and moral philosophy that derived from the humanistic tradition of Europe.

By a happy chance the British had moved the colonial capital from Jamestown to the college town of Williamsburg. Jefferson, along with the other students, was thus able to attend the meetings of the Burgesses, followed by the sessions of the General Court. Through his friends he knew the members of the Governor's Council. During the "public times" he attended the theater performances, danced at the balls, and talked with the delegates and lawyers about the moot issues of the day. Williamsburg was for him, as Dumas Malone has suggested, not only a way of learning the intellectual tradition, but a school of manners and a political listening post. Together the college and the capital formed an unparalleled training ground for statesmanship, an engine for transforming young men of birth and promise into leaders of the colony and (as it turned out) of the emerging nation. What the massive universities of Europe and America are straining to do today, with their far more complex mixture of human material of diverse origins, this tiny disorganized college, housed in a few brick buildings in a colonial village capital, was able to do without sweat and strain for a handful of young men who danced, gambled, grumbled, had college rows—and somehow shaped themselves into a great governing generation.

But if Jefferson learned from both the college and the capital he learned even more from a trio of men—William Small, George Wythe, and Francis

Fauquier. Small was a Scotsman, only nine years older than Jefferson, M. A. fresh out of Aberdeen, professor of mathematics, natural philosophy, and the sciences, and when the chair of moral philosophy fell vacant he doubled in that. It was one of those happy accidents when the right student and right teacher meet, and something happens in the younger man that changes him forever. The two spent all their available time together, so that in effect Small was Jefferson's private tutor—or perhaps better, they formed an apprentice-master relation, the best possible kind of learning arrangement. Jefferson wrote in his *Autobiography* that Small had "a happy talent of communication, correct and gentlemanly manners, and an enlarged and liberal mind. He, most happily for me, became soon attached to me and made me his daily companion when not engaged in the school; and from his conversation I got my first views of the expansion of science, and of the system of things in which we are placed."

Small opened for Jefferson the world of European intellectual experience. As it happened he came from Scotland exactly at the time when Scottish intellectual life had entered upon a Renaissance, and when Scottish thinkers—Francis Hutcheson, David Hume, William Robertson, Adam Smith—were dazzling the younger men not only in Britain, but throughout Europe. He had a bent for science, which he communicated to Jefferson, but behind it there was the thinking embodied in Scottish moral philosophy, with Hutcheson in the lead, and with a stress on private judgment based on available evidence in all moral and political matters. Benjamin Franklin had come into touch with this movement of thought when he visited Edinburgh and spent some time with Lord Henry Homes Kames, who had written on "natural religion."

Now young Jefferson became exposed to it. A self-reliant, sturdy young man, Small was something of a teaching rebel. For the old method of recitation by rote he substituted the lecture system; for the tension of hostile discipline imposed by the faculty he substituted an easy cordiality. He came under faculty attack, remained in Williamsburg only six years, and returned to Britain, where he was helpful to James Watt in the development of his steam engine. But the young Scotsman, who cared passionately about mathematics and science and their practical applications, left an enduring mark on his Virginian student, and gave strong support to his investigative bent.[1]

Through Small the young student was brought into touch with two other men who helped shape the bent of his talent—the principal legal scholar of Virginia, George Wythe, and the Lieutenant Governor and ranking British official in Virginia, Francis Fauquier. The three older men often dined together, usually at the Governor's palace, and young Jefferson felt lucky to share their conversation. Wythe was an important lawyer, a man not only of legal scholarship, but of a classical learning approaching pedantry. Fauquier, very different, was a man of the world in his fifties, an accomplished amateur at many things, including music, the study of the weather—and gambling. But his strength lay in Edmund Burke's "unbought grace of life," in food and drink and entertainment, in an urbanity of mind and elegance of manner that got him warmly received as governor in a restive colony, and in a style of Renaissance versatility, which his young friend may have caught from him.

When young Jefferson came to choose a profession he turned, not surprisingly, to the law, since it fitted into the interest evoked in him by the political and legal life of the colonial capital. Rather than going to the Inns of Court, in England, as some young Americans of his social rank did, he preferred to stay in America. He afterward generalized this decision, and he was to wage a protracted campaign against having young Americans go abroad for their professional studies; but along with this budding cultural nationalism there was at the time the practical fact of a good master being available to him. In the fashion of the time he read law as an apprentice with Wythe; he was deeply influenced by "Coke on Littleton," on the crucial theme of landed property law, as well as by the other textbook volumes in Edward Coke's *Institutes*; he briefed a number of the cases in two "Commonplace Books"—notebooks in which the young law apprentice shaped a kind of legal case method of his own, long before James Barr Ames and C. C. Langdell at Harvard Law School.

The young lawyer practiced the legal arts for seven years, until he was thirty. It was a successful and effective career at the bar. True, he had neither the deep erudition of Wythe nor of Thomas Mason, nor the fiery courtroom eloquence of Patrick Henry, who more than made up in charisma and emotional power for what he lacked in legal learning. Jefferson's voice was weak, his courtroom manner diffident and unaggressive. Yet, he had an authentic legal brilliance, with his lucid style and the economy and authority of his mind. In a single year he tried some four hundred cases, mostly small ones before the county courts, where he established invaluable relationships with the laymen magistrates, thus building a base for his later political career; and he also practiced before the General Court and made abstracts of its cases, along with the leading British decisions of his day, to serve as guides for colonial law. It was his legal training that enabled him, in an essay written in 1764 ("Whether Christianity is a Part of the Common Law") and in a later famous letter to John Cartwright, to offer a legal base for that separation of church and state which was dear to him. But one should add, as Gilbert Chinard has done, that his English common-law studies gave his thought an empiric and even conservative bent.

He was clearly one of the rising young men of the colony, adept not only in council, but in the elegance of the living style he was adopting. Even in his years as a lawyer he had not ceased to be a planter, keeping an eye on his estates and on his family. He began to build at Monticello, studying the chaste and austere formal style of the Italian architect Andrea Palladio, and of his English disciples, and applying it to the protracted process of designing and building his own house as an amateur of the arts. The man who was to call for a periodic revolutionary refreshment of liberty had a precise and orderly life-style of his own: from one angle the role of revolution, in his thinking, was to remove the artificial obstructions of tyranny and restore man to his "natural order." He courted and married an attractive young widow of a prosperous family, Martha Wayles Skelton, gave up his legal practice, and settled down in a wing of his unfinished house to the peaceful life of an accomplished country gentleman.[2]

But he was not to pursue it for long. The tensions in imperial relations between the colonies and Great Britain were mounting. Jefferson became, at twenty-five, a member of the Virginia House of Burgesses, joining in the company of colonial leaders who were increasingly engaged in a struggle with the mother country over trade, taxes, colonial autonomy, and the "rights of freeborn Englishmen." Jefferson had not yet become a rebel, but the role he played in deliberation with small groups of his colleagues (he never shone in open public debate) helped him to test and sharpen some of the principles he was later to apply to the theory and art of rebellion. A small group of younger men, with Jefferson, Patrick Henry, and Richard Henry Lee as leaders, began to meet informally at the Raleigh Tavern and set up the first colony-wide Committee of Correspondence, to keep in touch with patriots in other colonies and achieve some unity of action. He read John Locke and Montesquieu intensively at this time, and the fruits of his reading and thought were evident in a twenty-three-page pamphlet he drew up—*A Summary View of the Rights of British America*—for the Virginia delegation to present to a colonial Continental Congress held in Philadelphia in 1774.

The ground that Jefferson took in this widely read and quoted pamphlet was high and radical ground: that the colonies denied any authority in the British Parliament over them; that in the early colonial charters there was a compact between colonies and king; that they acknowledged the authority of the king as co-equal sovereignties along with England—as "having the same executive chief but no other necessary political connection"; in short, that the colonies were part of what the British empire was later to become after Lord John George Lambton Durham's report—a "commonwealth of nations." This was radical ground to take—too radical for a number of the older and more wary colonial leaders. It went beyond the Stamp Act and the other specific colonial grievances to the question of basic imperial relations.

After taking part in the Virginia assembly, where he backed up Patrick Henry's resounding call to arms, with its famous "Liberty or Death" peroration, Jefferson spent ten days making the journey of over three hundred miles to Philadelphia, where another Continental Congress was trying to give direction to the colonial military resistance after Bunker Hill. There he first met Benjamin Franklin, and began what was to prove a long friendship with John Adams, who noted the Virginian's "reputation for literature, science, and a happy talent for composition." Again Jefferson took little part in the general debates, but was effective on the small drafting committees. Despite his youth he was becoming the propaganda and manifesto expert of the little band of revolutionaries, their spokesman to the world, and a master of the war of ideas. While at Philadelphia he also drafted, in June, a constitution for his own Commonwealth of Virginia. Scholarship suggests that while it came rather late, it was debated, and some of its features (including the preamble) adopted. Yet the crucial reforms Jefferson suggested in it were not adopted—the idea of every man having land and an equal vote, the phased liquidation of slavery, the abolition of primogeniture and entail, and the guarantee of religious freedom.

Jefferson was clearly an earnest young revolutionary, committed to a meaningful internal democracy and freedom as well as to independence from Great Britain. He continued to fight for these reforms in the Assembly, until he pushed through the statute for religious freedom, which he drafted and in which he took an inextinguishable pride, but even at his death, fifty years later, he was still critical of the state constitution. Meanwhile, his preamble to it, indicting King George III for his acts of misrule, had an important meaning in his development—that of taking the critical step of repudiating the ties of the colonies with the British monarch as well as with the British Parliament.

He was now ready for his great task of political composition—the drafting of the Declaration of Independence. The decision to draw up this manifesto was made by the delegates on 7 June 1776, and a committee of five was chosen to prepare it, with Jefferson representing the Virginia delegation. By the common consent of the other members of the committee, he composed the first draft. He wrote it in seventeen days, between 11 June and 28 June, consulting (he later said) no books or pamphlets, but using the indictment of George III contained in his own Virginia preamble. Showing his draft first to Adams and Franklin, he then submitted it to the other committee members. It was debated by the Congress as a whole during three days, 2 July through 4 July, while Jefferson listened in silence, but doubtless in agony, as his prized sentences were dissected, while Franklin told him jokes meant to console him. Although Jefferson felt that his draft had been weakened in the course of the debate, the judgment of history has been that it was stripped of some of its excesses both in language and thought. It has become the most famous state paper in American history, embodying in brief span the essentials of American libertarian thinking and laying a base upon which Americans were to build much of the structure of their democratic theory.

Jefferson had been prepared for this task by his apprenticeship in drafting political manifestos as a rebellious Virginian, by the day-to-day ordeals that he and his fellow revolutionaries endured and which sharpened his thought and pen, but above all by his reading and reflection, and his alertness to the currents of thought and feeling around him. He was a child of the Enlightenment, and it was the doctrines of the Enlightenment—honed to a fine edge in the intensity of the revolutionary struggle—which he embodied in the Declaration.

"Where Jefferson got his ideas," Carl Becker wrote in his classic study, *The Declaration of Independence: A Study in the History of Political Ideas* (1922), "is hardly so much a question as where he could have got away from them." It is true that the ideas Jefferson drew upon were part of the climate of opinion of the time, and lay all about him. He said of his own purpose: "Not to find out new principles, or new arguments, never before thought of...but to place before mankind the common sense of the subject, in terms so plain as to command their assent."

Yet no one before him had ever given this "common sense" a form at once so sharp and sweeping, so concrete in example, and so universal in essence, as he did in the Declaration. Abraham Lincoln came closer to doing justice to it than either Becker or Jefferson himself. "The principles of Jefferson," Lincoln wrote in 1859, "are the definitions and axioms of free society. ...All honor to Jefferson—to the man who, in the concrete pressure of a struggle for national independence by a single people, had the coolness, forecast, and capacity to introduce into a merely revolutionary document, an abstract truth, applicable to all men and all times, and so to embalm it there, that to-day, and in all coming days, it shall be a rebuke and a stumbling-block to the very harbingers of re-appearing tyranny and oppression." The "merely revolutionary" occasion might have evoked a prosaic document or a shrill and bombastic one. The "abstract truth" was universal, which is why it has proved enduring.

Its crucial elements were the idea of an orderly natural universe as the expression of the divine principle, and therefore, a body of natural rights deriving from this universe ("the laws of nature and of nature's God"); the right of revolution against tyranny as one of these natural rights, and the basing of government on the "unalienable" rights of "life, liberty, and the pursuit of happiness." Add to these the doctrine not of a simplistic equality, but of equal access to equal life chances that must be accorded to every individual ("all men are created equal"). Add also the belief in the people themselves as the source of power (popular sovereignty) and as the only possible principle of government (majority rule). Add finally the common body of human values that are the possession of every people in the human family ("a decent respect to the opinions of mankind"), and of every era: hence, the concern with "posterity" which characterized the thinkers of the Enlightenment.

Parallel to these tenets there were other doctrines of the Enlightenment that are implied rather than explicitly cited in the Declaration: the reliance upon an expanding body of sciences that would illumine the workings of the natural universe, the existence of laws in history and in government as well as in the physical universe, the belief in human progress and in man's perfectibility, and the underlying conviction that if governments leave men alone—in their economic and political lives and in their worship of God in whatever way they choose—this principle of freedom will harmonize with the principle of order in the universe, and that the life goals common to all communities will thus be best fulfilled.

These were the ideas. But more than anything of a sustained character that Jefferson ever wrote the Declaration is also a superb achievement in style—in the matching of literary form to intellectual content and in this case political function. What gives it this style is its union of order and ardor, with a measured grace to accord with the weightiness of the occasion, but also with a fire of passion that keeps breaking through the frame of intellectual order and discipline. In *The Literary History of the American Revolution, 1763–1783* (1897), Moses Coit Tyler celebrates the Declaration as "a kind of war-song; it is a stately and passionate chant of human freedom," and few can doubt that it has had an evocative lyrical appeal ever since.

After declaring the independence of the colonies from Great Britain, the task of the revolutionary elite was a double one: first, to translate their defiant manifesto into the reality of freedom and sovereignty; and second, to build a new structure of unity and government. During the decade that followed the Declaration Jefferson was more closely involved with the second than with the first.

The draft of a Constitution for Virginia, mentioned earlier, did not arrive at Williamsburg in time, but his preamble was used. Jefferson was not happy about the state constitution that was adopted: it stripped the governor too radically of his executive authority and of his power of appointment; it did not provide a broad enough base of popular suffrage, using a stricter property qualification than Jefferson desired, since basically he believed in giving the suffrage to all white males; nor did it adopt Jefferson's proposal for separating church from state and doing away with the church establishment, nor his proposal for ending the importation of slaves.

But Jefferson continued his struggle against the continuance of the entrenched power of the aristocracy in the newly emerging American states. He introduced in the Virginia Assembly a bill against entails in the inheritance of landed estates. His opposition to both entails and primogeniture was crucial in the movement for abolishing restrictions on the inheritance of land, which was to form part of the social revolution that ran parallel to the anti-Colonial revolution. His attitude derived from his desire to free people from the dead hand of the past in the domain of land tenure, and thereby to provide economic opportunity for the disinherited and even land for the landless. Jefferson did not take a hostile position to the institution of property, but he wanted to strip entrenched privilege away from it, and open the acquisition of property to all. In his later development he became anticapitalist in the sense of regarding the plutocracy of urban manufacturers and note-holders as hostile to freedom. Yet, in his basic attitude toward land tenure he expressed the spirit of openness to new enterprise and popular energies that was later to become the dynamic element in the development of American capitalism.

It was Jefferson's ironic fate to become governor of Virginia under the constitution of whose provisions he was so skeptical, and to act dubiously in a war whose rationale he had set down so indelibly. He was elected governor in June, 1779 by the two legislative houses, and served for two years—a tenure of executive office which was in many ways the unhappiest of Jefferson's whole public career. His term of office was filled with the turmoil of a Commonwealth at war, which had to provide soldiers and arms for the Revolutionary army, had to deal with the wavering loyalties of the Indians in the back country, and had to find fiscal support for the extraordinary military expenses in an economy that had plenty of tobacco, but was stripped of hard money. The worst episode came when troops from an invading British fleet, with Benedict Arnold in command, entered the Virginia capital soon after Jefferson and his government had left in some haste, abandoning munitions, stores, and archives. The spectacle of the Virginia legislators, as well as the governor, retreating rather hastily and in disorder before a band of nine hundred British troops, and of the whole colony falling to it, was not a glorious one in the Revolutionary annals.

Jefferson was later called to account for his weakness of leadership by the assembly, mainly for not acting to forestall the landing of troops, and for failing to give General Friedrich Wilhelm von Steuben strong enough and early enough support. The fact was that the governor's office was at best a creature of the General Assembly, and that the lack of decisiveness lay not so much with the governor (although Jefferson proved to be far from a brilliant administrator), but with the distribution of powers in the Commonwealth. Jefferson relinquished his office at the end of his term, yielding it to a military governor, with a cloud of criticism accompanying his exit.

Every great man has at some point in his life an episode of bottomless despair, and this experience as war governor was Jefferson's. His enemies, then and later, hurled the charge of cowardice at him, and a modern Virginia historian, Hamilton J. Eckenrode, has blamed his Rousseauist mentality for leaving a mark of indecision on him. It was true of most of the creative leaders of the American revolution that they showed skill in political and propaganda tactics, but—except for Washington, Hamilton, and a few others—they were not impressive in facing the harsh realities of actual warfare. Jefferson might of course have pushed the issue of his executive power more persistently than he did. It was true that he didn't have the power to act decisively, but it was also true that he didn't ask the legislature for it. There was considerable talk, among the revolutionaries, of the need for a military constitutional dictatorship, but the very thought of it appalled Jefferson. Out of the turmoil of his experience as governor, he emerged a saddened man, eager to return to his Monticello estate and relinquish the care of public office.

But Jefferson was incapable of any real withdrawal. He used what leisure he could spare from his immediate political duties in an elaborate answer to a set of queries by the Marquis Francois de Barbe-Marbois on the state of Virginia—an answer that was to become the famous *Notes on the State of Virginia,* the only book that Jefferson ever wrote, which was to be used by generations of commentators on America (including Alexis de Tocqueville) as the most considerable and striking contemporary description of a single American state. Part of it was descriptive geography (on the mountains and rivers), part natural history (on the soil, the minerals, the animals), part the reflections of a sensitive and accomplished man of many talents upon the political and social institutions, as well as upon the look, expanse, and feel of the greatest of the American commonwealths. There was a spaciousness in the book that matched the spaciousness of Virginia, which (while Jefferson was writing his *Notes*) offered and ceded to the Confederacy the interior stretch that was to become West Virginia and Kentucky. He also added to his *Notes* a new draft of a constitution for Virginia, which stressed the separation of powers, but also stressed the dangers of legislative encroachment both on the executive power and upon the freedoms of the people.

The fact that his wife Martha had been in poor health worried Jefferson while he was away from home during the sessions of the Continental Congress at Philadelphia and of the assembly at Williamsburg. In ten years of marriage she bore him six children, although only two were to reach maturity. After her sixth child she failed rapidly, and died on 6 September 1782. Jefferson was plunged into grief, and for several months was unable to concentrate on any work. Just before the war ended he dallied with the idea of going to Paris as a member of the peace negotiating commission, but nothing came of it. He spent some time arranging his growing library (in 1783 it consisted of almost three thousand volumes) under a new scheme of classification.

After the signing of the peace treaty with Great Britain, on 3 September 1783, the insistent problem of the newly liberated commonwealths was to achieve a structure of unity. Jefferson's views were strongly in the unionist direction. Elected a member of the Continental Congress, which met at Annapolis, he urged an end to the prolonged disputations and debates ("our body was little numerous but very contentious") and helped round up enough of the straggling state delegations to get the Articles of Confederation confirmed by nine states.

When the new Congress accepted Virginia's gift of land, Jefferson headed the committee that drafted a plan for the future government of this territory, known as the Ordinance of 1784, which formed the nucleus of the later Ordinance of 1787, and which established the prime principle that new states carved out of the western territory should be admitted to the Union on the same terms as the original states. He had strongly urged the abolition of slavery and a ban on hereditary titles as conditions for admission, but Congress struck out both provisions. His term in the Congress also gave him a chance to work out a decimal system of coinage.

On 7 May 1784 he was chosen to join John Adams and Benjamin Franklin, who were already in Europe as ministers plenipotentiary, to build diplomatic fences for the new confederation by treaties of trade and friendship. The members of Congress expected Jefferson to bring his highly practical sense, as well as his extraordinary command of languages, to this task. Jefferson, at forty-one when he set sail from Boston on the *Ceres* with his daughter Patsy, his violin, and the manuscript of his *Notes on the State of Virginia,* was still a relatively young man, on the threshold of his full intellectual powers. The dark period of his life, when he had passed through the shadows of his Virginia governorship

and his wife's death, was behind him. After a brief fallow perio
plunged again into work, and his committee work and state p
the Congress were testimony to his new release of energies.

He was going to Europe with a sense of sharp expectancy, nc
a commissioner to bring back some treaties of commerce but al
modest way, as an intellectual and moral emissary from An
Europe. The years in Europe—more than five years from July
October, 1789—were to prove not only exciting in experi
achievement, but the most fruitful preparatory period for wha
to come in his career. They tested Jefferson as a democrat an
tionary, broadened him as an observer, refined him as a man of 1
turned him into a diplomat with an expanded horizon of wor
and deepened him as a thinker and statesman.

Notes

1. One may note that James Watt's steam engine and Adam Smith's *T*
   Nations, both associated with the Scottish school of intellectuals, w
   veiled in 1776, the same year as the Declaration of Independence
   drafted by a young American whom the liberating influence of the
   naissance and the European Enlightenment had managed to reach i
   ginia college town.
2. There was a brief earlier episode when the young bachelor paid cou
   to the wife of one of his best friends while the latter was away fro
   episode for which Jefferson was to express public regret much late
   came a political *cause célèbre.*

2

A Diplomat in Europe, 1785–1789

Looking back at Jefferson's life in perspective, we can see the creative role that the European years played in it; but in immediate terms they had their irritations and miseries. His first winter in Paris was a bleak one. He moved from quarters to quarters until he could find a house in Paris to his taste, but furnishing it was an expensive task (Congress refused to help), the salary of a minister was something less than munificent (two thousand guineas a year), and the difficulties of reliable communication with the States kept plaguing Jefferson. The monarchs, foreign ministers, state officials, and diplomats to whom Jefferson was formally presented were distant if polite, and the young diplomat felt that the American representatives were considered "the lowest of the diplomatic tribe." He could not be blamed if, for a time, he suffered a nostalgia for his native Virginia. He was lonesome for its sun, its rivers, its blue hills, its rustic elegance, its freedom from crowded cities and manufactures, its slow tempo of living.

Yet, in time the European experience grew on Jefferson. The frustrations and defeats that he suffered as a trade commissioner—whether with the French and British or the Portuguese or Algerians over the problem of Barbary piracy—receded into the background when Jefferson was chosen as minister to France to succeed Franklin. He succeeded in organizing his day in his new Paris home as closely as he could to his routines at Monticello, rising at six, breakfasting and working all morning with his secretaries, riding or taking long walks in the afternoon, browsing in the bookstalls to pick up the books for which he was so hungry, prowling the countryside around Paris with his insatiable curiosity about how the ordinary people lived.

As minister to France, Jefferson had the spotlight of public attention focused on him, much as had been true of Franklin. But, however much he admired Franklin as the only American revolutionary leader who could be placed in the same category with George Washington, his style—ambassadorial and personal alike—was not Franklin's, but his own. He had a small circle of American friends, especially young men like his secretary, William Short, and the artist John Trumbull, both of whom he treated like sons. His circle of French friends included the Marquis de Lafayette, the Duc de la Rochefoucauld-Liancourt, the philosopher Marquis de Condorcet, and others among the liberal intellectuals and nobility. He found the life of the more lighthearted part of Parisian society somewhat decadent, but he was strongly drawn to a small circle of American and French women who were part of the artistic life of the cosmopolitan community.

He had some sentimental interludes with several of them, particularly with Maria Cosway, the wife of a British miniaturist, to whom he wrote his famous letter, "Dialogue Between My Head and My Heart." After his wife's death, this was the period of Jefferson's life when he came closest to being carried away by a romantic attachment. But the lady was married, and Jefferson—for all the flowery language of his letters—was both scrupulous and wary, and nothing much came of the episode; when they met again in Europe at a later phase of their friendship, the earlier fires had died down. These were the only years of relative relaxation from the exacting pace of involvement with public life that Jefferson was to have until his retirement. One may guess that his dalliance with the little group of attractive and intelligent women cast a spell of enchantment over his whole European adventure.

There was drama, and even paradox, about the whole five-year sojourn in Europe. Here was this tall, loose-jointed American in Paris, anything but an innocent, in fact a distinguished world figure, yet he remained retiring and worked unobtrusively through others whenever he could, as notably in the negotiations over the tobacco monopoly. Here was a Virginia agrarian, who loved his hillside acres, living in the city most celebrated for its decadence. Here was a man who felt that political health resided with the independent farmer, identifying himself with a revolution led by the urban Third Estate and carried through by city mobs storming the Bastille and by street-fighters behind their ramparts of paving stones. Here was the defiantly native American who proved an indefatigable traveler, doing the sights of Europe, planning each foray like the surveyor's and explorer's son that he was, grasping the whole layout, studying the monuments, sketching the buildings that accorded best with his exactingly pure classical taste, trudging through farms and gardens and vineyards, taking in everything with an insatiable mind, a not-so-innocent eye, and a Faustian hunger for knowledge.

Here was one of America's polymaths and best amateur scientists— a stalwart of the Philosophical Society, a friend and correspondent of university Presidents—studying the weather wherever he went, taking the day's temperature readings, keeping elaborate notes on whatever he saw, visiting Comte Georges de Buffon and arguing with him about his provincial European views on American natural history, defending American animals and the American Indians against their European detractors, feeding information to any European who wanted to write on America or visit it, trying to set the factual record straight and correct distorted interpretations of his beloved country. Here was the unflagging utilitarian, more deeply stirred by an ingenious mechanical contrivance or utensil than by a sunset or painting or cathedral, sending back to America a straggling array of plants, trees, dogs, carriages, and gadgets that could be used or acclimatized in the new society; yet this gadgeteer missed the true meaning of the Industrial Revolution, which was coming into full swing in the Britain he visited, just as this scientist missed much of the importance of the scientific breakthrough going on in France.

Jefferson never ceased to be an American amidst his European travels and experiences. His European education was an intellectual and political overlay on his essential Americanism. He was an American revolutionary stationed in Paris, which was on the eve of a bloody revolution, wandering through a France whose society was still that of the *ancien régime*. He was an American humanist, immersed in the ancient world and its values, studying a Europe that was still in political chains, but beginning to question all ideas and values. Much of Jefferson's response to his European years marked less the intrusion of new insights and more the confirmation of his old views. He carried Virginia with him wherever he went. Perhaps he saw mainly what he wanted to see. "If anyone thinks," he wrote his friend George Wythe, "that kings, nobles, or priests are good conservators of the public happiness, send him here. It is the best school in the universe to cure him of that folly." The stupidity of Europe's kings ("I can...say with safety there is not a crowned head in Europe whose talents or merit would entitle him to be elected vestryman by the people of any parish in America"), the superstitions on which its clergy fed, the unproductive privileges of its nobility, the poverty and ignorance of the European common man: these were what Jefferson saw and wrote home about, and doubtless what he had come prepared to see.

It would be interesting to compare his insights into the political sociology of Europe with those that Alexis de Tocqueville carried back from America almost a half-century later. The genius of the two men was very different: one of them a statesman and humanist, an articulator of his time and its moods, a kind of radar-perceiver of the tremors and rumblings in the world around him; the other an introverted student of history and society, with piercing insights into the springs of political behavior, and a prescience about where the democratic tide was carrying human society. It is no service to Jefferson's real talents to try to make out of him a clairvoyant political philosopher like Tocqueville. He was what he was: a broad-gauged, many-faceted man of his time, a talented political leader, a good social observer, a man with a flair for the ideas around him, and with a pen sharp enough to impale them for the centuries in unforgettable phrases.

A man transplanted for a time to a civilization not his own carries on an interior dialogue, to compare the two civilizations and come to terms with both. Jefferson seems to have carried on two dialogues during his European years. In one he weighed the merits of American and European political institutions and social mores, using his European observations as the basis of his letters across the ocean on the new American Constitution, and his American experience in advising his French friends on political and constitutional strategy. The other dialogue was on the theme of revolution: comparing the American and French revolutions, assessing their nature and tactics, and calculating what price in blood— if any—was too high to pay for freedom from tyranny. In these two interior dialogues the main intellectual content of Jefferson's European years was summed up.

His letters from France on the efforts to change the American government show Jefferson's strength did not lie in a realistic appraisal of governmental institutions. He was not as scholarly as James Madison, nor had he thought as deeply into the problems of the distribution of powers between the hub and the rim of the governmental wheel. Several times he praised the existing Confederation more highly than it deserved—perhaps because, as an American in Europe, he was overly defensive about American institutions. He felt out of the stream of the political action in America in that fateful year of 1787, when the newly independent states were assembling their best talents to revise their frame of government and turn themselves into an effective nation. Jefferson knew that he was a good political draftsman and at his best in the consultation of small groups, yet here he was in Europe, far away from the "assembly of demi-gods," as he called the Constitutional Convention.

No wonder he felt frustrated and anxious, especially since it took months for an exchange of letters with his friends across the ocean. He thought (wrongly, as we now see) that it was a mistake to keep the deliberations of the Convention secret. He chafed at the fact that his friend Madison was so strangely close-mouthed in his letters about the Constitution-making process. He feared the overcentralizing of the federal power in providing for a president who (as he wrote Adams) "seems a bad edition of the Polish king." He felt that the fears of the people, engendered especially by Shay's Rebellion, might move the framers of the Constitution to go too far toward institutions that might become instruments of tyranny such as he saw around him in Europe. "Our Convention," he wrote an American correspondent, "has been too much impressed by the insurrection in Massachusetts." When he saw the draft of the Constitution some of his anxieties were allayed, and he saw "a great mass of good in it...but...also to me a bitter pill or two." The issue even strained his relations with Madison, but when they exchanged long, temperate letters about the Constitution, the two friends came close to an understanding.

Their difference was one of emphasis, but an important one. To Jefferson the crucial problem in government was one of safeguarding the liberties of the people from potential tyrannies; to Madison it was one of finding, empirically as well as theoretically, the pattern of power and safeguards that would provide effective government. Because Madison and Alexander Hamilton had a common belief in *energetic* government, they were able to write *The Federalist Papers* together, although they had been opposed on specific issues in the Convention itself and had divergent political values. Madison was probably more concerned about the freedoms of the people than Hamilton was. But he felt that the real danger to those freedoms sprang not from too much, but from too little and too ineffectual power in the government: when there is too little power, he wrote Jefferson, "the abuses of liberty beget a sudden transition to an undue degree of power"—or, in the language of our own day, it is governmental collapse and chaos rather than governmental energy which bring totalitarianism. Jefferson was never wholly convinced by this reasoning, nor by the whole stress of *The Federalist* authors upon energetic government: "I own," he wrote Madison, "that I am not a friend to a very energetic government. It is always oppressive."

Madison had the advantage of being in the thick of things, with a radar that could catch the anxieties of all sections and classes about a government which was simply not functioning with energy because it lacked adequate power. He saw that in any federal structure the central government cannot negotiate with the states nor keep going back to them for a renewal of its mandate, but must operate directly on the people of all the states and draw its powers from them by a single original grant. Once this principle was accepted, the rest followed: the voting in Congress not by states but by members, the grant of the tax-levying powers to the federal government, the apportionment of representatives in the lower House by population, the office of the president. Reporting the intense Convention debates he had also gauged the resistances to the new approach, and had been part of the brilliant compromises by which diverse classes and regions had found a synthesis for their interests.

What sort of role would Jefferson have played had he been at the Convention? Perhaps the urgencies of time and place would have weighed almost as heavily with him as with Madison, but it is unlikely. It would have been strange if the author of the Declaration of Independence, with its deep radicalism of principle, would have given his full support to the consolidation of national power in a conservative Constitution.

Even from a distance, however, he exerted an important influence. He had two final objections to the Constitution as it was framed. First, it did not provide for presidential rotation in office. But the integrity of Washington, as the inevitable first president, fended off what might have been more pressing and widespread anxieties of presidential self-perpetuation in office. The tradition of self-limitation operated until Franklin Roosevelt's four terms, and then a constitutional amendment put it into legally binding terms. On his other objection Jefferson was militant and unreconstructed: "A bill of rights," he wrote Madison, "is what the people are entitled to against every government on earth, general or particular, and what no just government should refuse, or rest on inferences." Many others felt as he did; even John Adams, also in Europe, had written earlier to Jefferson asking, "What think you of a Declaration of Rights? Should not such a thing have preceded the model?" It was Jefferson, however, who was the prime influence in the movement for a Bill of Rights. He kept up the pressure through correspondence and through his allies at home until the Constitution was ratified. Then the first ten Amendments were voted as a kind of *condition subsequent* rather than a *condition precedent* to the Constitution. Aside from anything else he may have done in his career, this role of championing the Bill of Rights— along with the authorship of the Declaration—justifies Jefferson's claim as the greatest of American libertarians.

All this time Jefferson was watching the effort of the French to topple the *ancien régime* and replace it with a more democratic political and social structure. Here Jefferson was a moderate, identifying with the French reformers who wanted to bring the Third Estate into the government, and to limit the privileges of nobles and clergy as well as the power of the monarchy. Jefferson identified with the more liberal of the aristocrats who called themselves the "Patriots," like his friend the Marquis de Lafayette, and with intellectuals like Condercet. As a diplomat he refused at first to give explicit advice, but at one point he did meet with Lafayette and a group of his friends in a long session on Constitution making. He even prepared a draft of a Charter of Rights, which he hoped the king (Louis XVI) would present to all the Estates, providing for a constitutional monarchy. He was fearful of bloody repression if the concessions were not granted and accepted, and felt that gradualism was the only approach for the French. But things moved fast and after the Tennis Court oath and the merging of the three orders the Assembly became dominant. Jefferson did not lose hope: he effected an orderly process of constitution making, and even counseled Lafayette on the wording of a Bill of Rights. But again, events moved faster than Jefferson had counted on. The fall of the Bastille, the surrender of the king, the flight of the princes, the spread of the peasants' revolt throughout France, the burning of the chateaux—the rapid succession of these events upset Jefferson's positions almost as soon as he took them.

At each turn of the revolution Jefferson moved along after it, approving it because of its general direction. But he was far from prescient about how rapidly or how far it would go. What moved him most was the conviction that the French were finally playing their role in an era of revolutions for Europe as for America. That is why he exulted over the Declaration of Rights, toward the end of August, 1789, and felt pride in the fact that America had shown the way in "the appeal to the rights of man." Jefferson was primarily an ideologist, and it was in this role, rather than as a tactician, that he felt most at home.

However great Jefferson's prestige may have been with the more rational and reflective of the French liberal leaders, he did not exert any appreciable influence on the course of the Revolution. Nor did he break through to the underlying forces that were shaping the Revolution: he was a champion and ideologist of revolutions, not a student of revolutions and how they take their course. Someone has said that Jefferson knew how to feel with his mind and to see with his heart. It was a double-edged compliment. Jefferson was one of the illustrious intellectuals and one of the shrewdest diplomats and statesmen of his era, but he was not a disciplined social thinker. Exactly because he believed in the progress of mankind and was sensitive to the aspirations of his time, he was bound to have illusions about the course of revolutions.

This inner dialogue had to be suspended when Jefferson made plans to sail for America in the fall of 1789. He thought he was only getting a leave of absence, to enable him to put some of his affairs in order at home, but on the day he left Paris, 26 September 1789, his nomination as Secretary of State in the new federal government was approved by the Senate. He left behind him a striking record as an American envoy. He had carried on delicate negotiations with Comte de Vergennes, the French foreign minister, over the abolition of the tobacco monopoly in France, which bore heavily on American tobacco growers and shippers. He had obtained concessions from the French on American commerce. Along with John Adams, he had done effective work in renegotiating American credit with new bankers in Amsterdam. He had also negotiated with the new foreign minister, Comte de Montmorin, a consular convention that gave the fledgling nation new diplomatic prestige as well as protection against discriminations in commerce. Aside from these concrete achievements, he had made an exemplary record in his official and human relations, avoiding the temptation to intervene in the turmoil of a people in the early stages of a revolution, and establishing the image of an America whose envoys (Jefferson followed Franklin) were not intellectual barbarians, but men of sophistication, taste, and scientific curiosity.

It is not easy to describe the multifaceted contradictory figure who was the Thomas Jefferson of 1789, about to return to Virginia. He was a radical in his political thinking and feeling, a liberal optimist in his historical vision, a moderate in his tactics and the tactical advice he gave his French friends, an aristocrat in his friendships, a republican in the simplicity of his clothes and manners, a romantic in his revolutionary identifications, a realist in diplomacy, a mercantilist with free-trade residues in his economic thinking, a classicist in his architectural style, a revisionist in religion, and a traditionalist in ethics.

3

The Struggle for National Mastery, 1789–1800

Jefferson came home to the acclaim of his neighbors, with general approval of his appointment. The nation was lucky to have in Washington, Jefferson, and Hamilton a ruling triumvirate whose ability and distinction matched the comparable governing elite of any of the older nations of Europe. Washington was the only man—after Franklin's death—for whom Jefferson had a touch of awe. Whatever his limitations of subtlety and intellect, he had an unparalleled integrity and strength of character, a balanced judgment, and a quality of unquestioned command that came out of his war experience and the charisma surrounding a great national hero. Hamilton had a brilliant intellect, a sure orientation to power, a long-range vision of what was required in the process of nation making, and a capacity to seize upon any subject—whether war, monetary and financial policy, or foreign affairs—and master its principles and tactics. What Jefferson added to these two was his flair for ideas, feeling for the mood of a people and era, his mastery of phrase, and a weighty sense of strategy and decision making in foreign policy. This trio presented a formidable array of talents, working together well because each of the two younger men admired the president, while Washington in turn knew how to keep the two adversaries in harness, making use of the special talents of each, and getting a fuller resonance for his administration because of the counterpoint that each provided.

Some biographers have emphasized the rivalry between Jefferson and Hamilton, and the historian is tempted to treat the whole period as a kind of dueling contest. But viewing American history as the record of the national will, and American government as an energy system, one must note not only the rivalry, but the way the new nation now reaped its harvest of leadership. The governing elite had been trained in a series of sessions at a hard school: in the anticolonial agitation and struggle, in the war itself, in the period of governmental trial following it, in the process of Constitution making and foreign negotiation, in the constant debates and letter writing and public discussion. Because it was a hard school it was a school for statesmen. Jefferson had served in all its successive sessions, and had learned from each a new element of insight, of command, of self-mastery. Now during his tenure as secretary of state—for almost four years from March, 1790 to the end of 1793—he served the first president as his first secretary, dealing with issues of domestic as well as foreign policy. Not only did he turn his past experience to use in shaping one of the great administrations in American history, but his experience in that administration in turn prepared him for the decisions he had to take later as president.

It was not a happy period in Jefferson's life, and its last year was so wearying that Jefferson came to feel about the secretaryship something of the fatigue—plus aversion—he had felt for the Virginia governorship. He worked with only a staff of four or five, including messengers and translators, and with a total departmental budget (at the start) of $8,000, which included his own salary of $3,500. Dealing with a diplomatic corps that scarcely existed yet, and with American envoys and consuls who were just being sent abroad, he had also to run an odds-and-ends department to which were entrusted the administrative chores that didn't fall under others—including the Mint, the administration of patents (which Jefferson got off to a brilliant start), weights and measures (his proposal for a uniform decimal system failed), and the communications of the federal government with the state governors.

Jefferson felt he had to attend the state dinners and the rather formidable levees that George Washington held at his initial awkward court. But he fought the efforts (which were futile, as the events proved) to establish titles and rituals on the republican American soil. John Adams, who was in reality no monarchist although he sometimes talked like one, was the prime force behind these efforts; but he had Washington's agreement. Adams saw early what Walter Bagehot was to point out much later in *The English Constitution* (1867)—that the trappings of government were those symbolic elements by which men live as much as they live by power and self-interest. Adams's mistake was to generalize from the British experience: he failed to see the spirit of a civic religion among

Americans which had already begun to form around a commitment to democratic freedom plus social order, although it had not yet crystallized in the later cult of the Constitution.

Jefferson and Hamilton worked at the start in effective (although somewhat uneasy) harness. Jefferson was forty-seven at the time, Hamilton a remarkably mature and self-confident thirty-three, and each at the height of his powers. But before long one detects the beginnings of Jefferson's animus against Hamilton and the conservatives in the new administration, and theirs against him—in short, the beginnings of a party split inside the national government of all the talents. The Claude Bowers approach [in his *Jefferson and Hamilton: The Struggle for Democracy in America* (1925)] has tended to overdramatize and oversimplify the conflict between them. It was not a personal conflict, not even a party conflict primarily, but a renewed phase of the earlier conflict between interest groups, between sections, ultimately between strategies for national development and basic world outlooks. One element of the larger struggle was the emerging personal struggle between the two men. Only when it is seen within the larger frame does this personal struggle take on meaning.

Washington himself tried to keep the split between the two men from getting too sharp, and he tried to deal justly with both, as between quarreling sons. In his own twilight years Jefferson paid a qualified tribute to Washington: "We knew his honesty," he was to write in 1814, almost a quarter-century later, "the wiles with which he was encompassed, and that age had already begun to relax the firmness of his purposes." The passage of time had not relaxed Jefferson's memory of Hamilton's "wiles." Jefferson never failed to see the element of political partisanship in Hamilton, which was there, but he minimized the stature of his statecraft, which was also there. Actually Hamilton was indispensable to Washington, who had a distaste for economics and finance and left them gladly to the brilliant young man with a flair for them. On the other hand, he was deeply absorbed with foreign policy, and while he gave Jefferson reasonable scope and respected his judgments, the survival of the young republic depended too crucially on its relations with England and France for the president to trust any man wholly, including one whose ideological commitment (anti-British, pro-French) was as strong as Jefferson's. On several occasions, as with the appointment of Gouverneur Morris as Ambassador and President Washington's approval of the commercial treaty with Great Britain, the president took over from Jefferson and in effect became his own secretary of state.

Jefferson took these presidential interventions in his stride, but he resented Hamilton's intrusions into foreign policy, always on the side of the British and at least once—as will be noted soon—in highly questionable secret collusion with a British agent. When the president asked Jefferson for his opinion on Hamilton's economic program, Jefferson not surprisingly expressed his opposition, especially to the assumption of debts by the federal government. Only later did Jefferson's criticisms become a conscious part of the determined Republican party drive against Hamilton and what he stood for. As a cabinet member, Jefferson was at a disadvantage because his reports were always to the president, to whom alone he was responsible, while Hamilton's were to the Congress: this gave the secretary of the treasury direct access to Congress which Jefferson had only indirectly through his friend James Madison, who became the effective leader of the House.

If it is too much to say, as some have done, that Hamilton was Washington's prime minister, there is little question that the president leaned toward his politics and approved his economics, and that the young secretary set the administration tone considerably more than Jefferson did. The Federalists were in the saddle, as Jefferson sadly felt, booted and spurred to ride the new nation. Hamilton was primarily the financial policymaker, but in these early years financial policy went to the heart of the nation's strength and growth. In his series of famous "Reports to Congress" on various phases of economic policy—on the assumption of debts and on public credit, on a Bank of the U.S., on the encouragement of manufactures—Hamilton spelled out not only a set of policies, but a "Grand Design" for national growth. The aim was to generate economic strength by funding the outstanding debts and making them federal debts; by establishing the new government's credit abroad and at home; by creating fluid capital; by setting up a protective tariff and beginning the process of industrializing an agrarian economy; and by tying the rising class of merchants, toolmakers, creditors, noteholders, bankers, and manufacturers to the fortunes of the new nation.

Hamilton was in this sense a nationalist economic planner along with being politically federalist and antipopulist. He had a flaring imagination, which fed on an ambitious program that would bring glory to America and himself. He thought of America in continental and imperial terms. But the key to empire for him was economic growth, as the key to glory was national strength, and the key to that in turn was a broad interpretation of Constitutional powers, a vigorous cultivation of banking and manufactures, and a confident course in foreign policy, including a clear federal power over war and peace, and the creation of an army-in-being. Unlike many of the European thinkers of his time, Hamilton did not believe in a universe where God's hidden hand kept the economy and policy in order: he believed, rather, in the vigorous supporting hand of government. Looking back at Hamilton in the light of later statesmen, one catches in him a hint of Benjamin Disraeli's incendiary imperial imagination, along with the English leader's activist Toryism. One catches also a little of Charles de Gaulle's cult of the nation, glory, the martial virtues, and the leadership role of the dominant personality. There are passages in Hamilton's letters that remind one of de Gaulle's conviction that the true leader does not wait for history to happen to him, but that he happens to history.

It is scarcely surprising that such a man and mind clashed with Jefferson. Where Hamilton was obsessed with centralized power and the danger of lack of "energy" in a government, Jefferson feared tyranny when located anywhere, thought it most likely that it would come from centralization, and was zealous for the liberties of the individual. Where Hamilton thought in terms of the glory of the nation, Jefferson thought (at least in his rhetoric) of the happiness of obscure men. Where Hamilton saw the Constitution as having to adapt itself to the needs of an expanding national power, Jefferson wanted the Constitution construed strictly, placing the burden of proof on any expansion of power not set down explicitly in the document. Where Hamilton felt that credit expansion would create capital and prosperity, Jefferson feared it would be used to corrupt the legislature and would only create a new aristocracy of paper. Where Hamilton favored a constant economic dynamism, Jefferson felt that economic growth would come better if it came steadily and healthily from skill and enterprise released from the oppressive hand of governmental tyranny. Where Hamilton, who had come of obscure birth and was wholly a self-made man, identified himself strongly with the new economic elites, Jefferson—born of a landed aristocracy—identified himself with the agrarian interest and the independent farmer and craftsman. Where Hamilton's Grand Design—it was nothing less—was of a thriving industrialized "Great Power," Jefferson's dream was of an agrarian republic of freemen, with whatever economic base it needed to prosper and be healthy. Where Hamilton romanticized the nation, Jefferson romanticized the people.

In his economic thought Jefferson was not a vigorous and original thinker, as Hamilton was, and perhaps John Adams and Madison. In their European days together he learned a good deal about economics from Adams which helped to shape his view, and after his return he learned even more from Madison: together the two political allies fashioned an economic theory and strategy to counter the strategy of Hamilton. The latter was quite genuinely dismayed that Madison, who had stood with him at the Constitutional Convention and later collaborated with him on *The Federalist Papers,* should now have turned against him. He assigned it to Jefferson's partisan influence. But the fact was that both Jefferson and Madison were very much alive to the political impact of Hamilton's measures, which were calculated to do a good deal for New York and New England merchants, but very little for the landed gentry or farm folk of the southern states.

They also had deeper reasons of economic policy and basic philosophy for opposing Hamilton. They were willing to support the funding and assumption of the debts on condition that a line be drawn between the original owners of the notes—most of them impoverished war veterans—and the later holders, many of whom had bought them up for speculation. Moreover, Jefferson as a politician feared that assumption on Hamilton's terms gave him too great a leverage with legislators who were not immune to the speculative fever that set in; while Jefferson as moralist recoiled from the idea of men getting rich on paper speculations without work of any sort, while farmers and craftsmen became the forgotten men. In the end they struck a compromise. Fearing that without the support of the Madison-Jefferson forces in Congress his whole economic program would be lost, Hamilton proposed a "deal" to Jefferson: if he could get funding and assumption on his terms, he would throw his support to the South's site for the new national capital—Washington City. Jefferson invited Hamilton and Madison to his house for dinner, and the deal was agreed upon. If it be not called a piece of crass opportunism, it was an early example of what one must call Jefferson's political flexibility.

Hamilton had the advantage of knowing exactly what he wanted. As noted earlier, his proposals for funding and assumption were part of a larger Grand Design, which included his policies on manufactures, industrialization, banking, and a clear position on the constitutionality of these measures, especially of a U.S. Bank. With no Grand Design of his own, Jefferson was necessarily more tentative in his economic views, and during the first year or two as secretary he felt his way toward viable policies that would square with his basic principles. The young republic faced the need for credit abroad, revenue and capital at home, and was confronted by discriminatory commercial practices on the part of the Great Powers in Europe. In this context there were no dividing lines between economic and commercial policy and foreign policy. In fact, in this period economic policy went to the very heart of foreign policy. This is why Jefferson reacted so strongly to Hamilton's treasury proposals, and why Hamilton in turn intervened so constantly in the conduct of foreign affairs.

Despite their differences of emphasis and their open conflicts, however, there was a concept broad enough to include the views of both—that of mercantilism, in the sense of a body of doctrine looking toward the total self-sufficient economic and political strength of the nation. Both Hamilton and Jefferson shared the belief that America had to break sharply with the economic hegemony of Europe, and develop a base for a self-sufficient economy of its own, which would make it economically independent of Europe after a revolution, which had made it politically independent. Mercantilism was the dominant mode of thinking of the time, in Europe as well as in America. But there were greater problems for the young nation than for the established ones, and necessity was in this case the prod for innovating thought on the part of the core group of American thinkers.

In economic terms mercantilism meant a sturdy growth and industrialization through bounties (which Hamilton favored) and protective tariffs (which he strangely neglected at the start, but which Jefferson and Madison favored). It also meant breaking through the European structure of economic discrimination. Jefferson had at one time believed in free trade, which suited the universalist and libertarian temper of his thought, but he came to understand that it was impossible to apply unless other nations applied it as well. Although he has often been called a Physiocrat, he was not—like John Taylor—a thoroughgoing and diehard member of the school, always determined to defend the landed and agrarian interest against a rising bourgeoisie. His bent was clearly toward an agrarian society, and as an ideal he never wavered from it. But as a matter of economic and political practicality, he not only did what he could to send gadgets and inventions home from Europe, he also found it necessary to support the encouragement of manufactures through protective tariffs, although it meant the growth of the city culture that he feared. He built a political alliance later between the planter, the farmer, and the city craftsman and worker.

It was because of these practical compromises that the group of southern agrarian intellectuals in the 1920s felt that Jefferson had betrayed the cause by departing from the Physiocratic doctrine, which defended the agrarian way of life. It has been suggested that Jefferson did not foresee the factory system and urban culture that were bound to accompany industrial technology and the development of manufacturing. It is fairer to say that Jefferson foresaw the consequences, but given his larger objectives—of a strong economy and a polity vigorous enough to remain free in the face of troubled European relations and hostile foreign strength—he saw no way to achieve it except by compromising his agrarian vision.

4

The Practice and Theory of Foreign Policy, 1789–1795

Jefferson had become, on the level of diplomacy, a skilled and seasoned professional negotiator who could match wits with the best emissaries the European nations sent and with the men who sat and pulled the policy strings in the European capitals.

It is a mistake to read back our own conceptual vocabulary about foreign policy into Jefferson's day, and try to decide whether he was an *isolationist* or *interventionist*. These terms, which are facets of a debate about how America should use its vast global power, were in the context of Jefferson's time almost meaningless. Charles Beard has called him a "continentalist," in the double sense that he aimed both at expanding American power as far as possible on the Continent and at keeping foreign powers out of it, and at the same time aimed at restricting American military action, if any, to the Continent. *Continentalist* is both descriptive and comprehensive, and is probably as good a term as any for Jefferson. My own preference, however, would be to call him an *ideological realist*: "ideological" because his overarching worldview informed his every act, "realist" because his base and test of policy were always brought back to the national interest, and because his methods were always tough minded.

When he carried on his difficult negotiations with the first minister whom the British sent to the United States, George Hammond, his concern was to make the strongest possible legal case on the British violations of the peace treaty, and the formal paper he drew, in response to Hammond's statement of the British case, is probably the subtlest and most vigorous document of his diplomatic career. Hammond, who was in constant touch with Alexander Hamilton at the time, and receiving advice from him about the best tactics to pursue with Jefferson, was baffled with the correct but unyielding policy with which the secretary of state confronted him. On the other hand, the French minister Jean-Baptiste Ternant, who had expected Jefferson to be compliant about the French position, felt himself equally baffled by his friendly but objective stance.

Jefferson as a diplomat did not make the mistake of confusing his own ideological sympathies with the American national interest. What he wanted from the French was the abandonment of their discriminatory trade policies toward the United States, and he knew that he could achieve it not by cozying up to them, but by hard bargaining, by holding over them the potential weapon of trade reprisals, and by keeping them guessing about American negotiations with the British. What he wanted from the British in turn was a definitive overall treaty that would settle the grievances carrying over from the original peace treaty, and which would settle the more recent commercial conflicts as well.

In his negotiations with both countries as secretary of state, Jefferson had his shining hour, not because the American cause was successful—it was only tolerably so—but because the taxing character of the problems compelled him to use every resource at his command. He achieved an objectivity as a statesman which set a difficult precedent for his successors in the secretary's post. The qualities that he brought to these negotiations could not have been found elsewhere in anything like the same combination: a mastery of detail, a capacity for cogent and persuasive marshalling of argument, an elegance of language, a subtlety of maneuver, and a basic strategic sense about the larger outlines of the American national interest.

To these should be added a skill in political warfare that Jefferson had in full measure. Like others in the new government, he was aware that the sinews of American strength did not lie in commerce or wealth or military power, but rather in the mythic quality of the American revolutionary victory, and the impact which the idea of America and its future had upon revolutionary thinkers and activists in Europe. Jefferson was not loath to practice political warfare with this ideological weapon. After the last legal argument had been made in his negotiations with the European powers—especially with the British and the Spaniards—and after both sides in the negotiations had invoked whatever weapons of economic strength they possessed, there remained the ideological weapon—and Jefferson was, of all men, the man who could best use it.

This does not mean that he was averse to using regular methods. In 1790, while the Spanish and British were involved in the Nootka Sound dispute over British ships on the Pacific coast, Jefferson seized the occasion to put pressure on the Spanish to yield to the United States all the territory east of the Mississippi. His fear was that, if Britain and Spain went to war, the Mississippi territory might be occupied by the British, which would be far more dangerous for American interests than the Spanish presence. As it turned out, Spain backed down in the Nootka Sound episode, and nothing came of Jefferson's power squeeze on the Mississippi territory. But he showed he was willing to use European embroilments for the American territorial interest even if—as in this instance—it might involve America in war.

One may say that Jefferson showed a quality of ruthlessness here which doesn't jibe with the usual portrait of him as a gentle liberal ideologist. But the truth was that while his objectives were those of a revolutionary democracy, and part of his reliance was on political warfare, Jefferson had learned his lesson well during his years in Europe—the lesson of a *real-politik* at which no European diplomat of the time was superior to him. In fact the great master of European diplomacy, Charles Maurice de Talleyrand, who was a contemporary of Jefferson, counted him as one of the great world figures of the time.

Jefferson's diplomatic objectives had a strong and disarming simplicity about them. They aimed to remove, or whittle down drastically, the commercial discriminations against the young republic on the part of all three of the great European powers; to open the Mediterranean Sea and the West Indies to American trade and shipping; to clear the Spanish, French, and British out of whatever control they had over commerce and navigation on the Mississippi, a cardinal geo-political factor in Jefferson's policy; to get the British out of the Western frontier posts, some of which they still held in defiance of the peace treaty, on the ground that British debts had not been paid and that several of the states had confiscated Loyalist lands; to open the west not only to commerce and navigation from the eastern states, but also to settlement, and thus to the creation of a home market for American products; to fashion an American policy of stringent neutrality in the struggles between the contending European powers, not allowing ideological preferences for the French or British cause to influence American actions; to use the European struggles as a shield of protection for the young nation by exploiting the vulnerabilities of each camp and playing each off against the other; and at the same time to help the world revolutionary cause and thus assure America's survival and greatness "among the nations of the earth."

These formed a program, a set of objectives, a body of tactics. They formed also an angle of vision from which to look out at the world and fashion a foreign policy whose concrete features would change in response to the shifting alignments and convulsive revolutionary changes in the world, but which would remain a cohesive and viable instrument amid these changes.

One of the products of Jefferson's basic foreign policy approach was not to come to fruition until 1795, after he had resigned as secretary of state. It was Pinckney's treaty with Spain, by which the United States gained free navigation of the Mississippi and a clear boundary demarcation and a settlement of other outstanding disputes. Still later, when he became president, Jefferson was to round out his Mississippi policy with the grand diplomatic achievement of his career, the Louisiana Purchase. So bent was he on the policy of American expansion to its natural frontiers, characteristically justified by a theory of natural rights, that he overrode all his constitutional objections to the use of implied powers by the federal government. Although Jefferson refused to break his political retirement in order to negotiate the treaty with Spain, as President Washington invited him to do, he gave the Pinckney Treaty his strong approval.

This was not true of the other important treaty of the Washington administration, Jay's treaty with Great Britain in 1795, which followed the Hamiltonian line of policy far more than the Jeffersonian. Except for the withdrawal of the British from the disputed northwest coasts, and the agreement to refer the dispute over American shipping losses to a commission, the treaty was heavily weighted on the side of the British demands. This was especially true in the repayment of American private debts to the British, and in a ten-year guarantee which the United States gave to the British against possible discriminations on tariffs and shipping. Jefferson was bitter at what he considered a humiliating surrender to the British. Hence, the newly emerging Republican party fought ratification by every possible means, including Congressional resolutions, stormy protest meetings, and even a mass demonstration in which a copy of the treaty was placed on a pole, carried through the streets, and burned in front of the residence of the British minister.

Jefferson's bitterness carried him to unrealistic limits. He felt that the self-denying ban against American tariff and tonnage discrimination needed not only the consent of the Senate, but the concurrence of both houses, and that the House should reject it. This interpretation would have crippled the treaty-making power of the president and the Senate, but it was not the only time that Jefferson as a partisan leader was swept into positions which would have made effective government difficult. But he was also objective enough to admire the "bold party stroke" which the treaty represented for Hamilton and his group, since it smoothed out the difficulties with Great Britain and allowed public attention to focus on the turbulence of events in France.

5

The Two Revolutions

During most of the decade of the 1790s, the shadow under which Jefferson had to work, think, and function as a political activist was the shadow of the French Revolution. Whatever doubts troubled him as he got reports from Paris about the fate of his friends—both among the liberal aristocrats and the intellectuals—who had been pushed out of the Revolution and imprisoned (as happened even to Lafayette in the end), Jefferson never faltered in identifying with the Revolution. Even when the execution of the French king (Louis XVI) brought with it a spreading Reign of Terror in Paris and the excesses of the jacquerie in the rural areas, Jefferson at first suspected that the reports had been exaggerated by the anti-French groups in Britain and America. When he could no longer doubt the extent of the revolutionary bloodshed, he fell back on his basic position—that while he deplored any aspects of the violence, it was better in the total span of history to have some deaths and injustices happen, and get them over and done with, than to have the mass of the people continue to suffer under despotism.

There is little question that Jefferson was initially an enthusiast for the French Revolution because he believed it would issue in a Gallic copy of the American Revolution. That was why he identified so strongly with his Paris friends, the liberal aristocrats and intellectuals, who formed later links with the Revolution through letters they exchanged with him. It was also why he favored retaining a liberalized French monarchy, scarcely dreaming that as the Revolution grew more intense it would suspend the monarchy and then abolish it and kill the monarch. It took Jefferson a while to rally from his gloom at these events, and to sustain his support of the Revolution.

But in reorienting his thinking he failed to see that this was not the revolution he thought it was at the start, but a drastically different type of revolution. It was no longer a Gallic copy of the American Revolution, or of the British success in turning an absolute monarchy into a constitutional one. Just as the monarchy as an institution had been swept away, so constitutionalism was being thrust aside as an irrelevance, because it hampered the further course of the Revolution. What took their place was the Revolution itself, with its own logic of power to those who could wield it in the name of the people, and its own mystique. We who have witnessed the later history of this idea of democratic totalitarianism, and its successive reincarnations in the Paris Commune of 1870, in the Leninist Revolution, in the "People's Democracies" of Eastern Europe, and in the Chinese Revolution, are able to get a perspective of it which was denied to Jefferson and his contemporaries.

The stand Jefferson took was not an easy one. It took courage as well as political zeal. When the French Revolution moved from its constitutional phase into the phase of the Terror, it caused a revulsion even among many sympathetic liberals, both in Europe and in America. Jefferson and his friends recognized the strength of this reaction, and thought of it as a counter-revolutionary swing in opinion. He was convinced that the Hamiltonian group would exploit this swing, and he and his friends did everything possible to meet and counter these tactics and to close their own ranks in the face of the adverse news. This closing of ranks involved a good deal of communication between the Republican leaders, both directly and by correspondence in order to clarify the party line of defense and attack.

It was here that Jefferson took the leadership and served his most useful function, as a master of tactic and persuasion, both through letters and through personal confrontation. For the most part he did not wait to defend the position of his group, but took the offensive. His letter to Philip Mazzei, written on 24 April 1796, a few months before being elected vice president—which was published in Europe and gleefully republished in the Federalist press in America and plagued Jefferson for some years—spoke of the rise of "an Anglican monarchical, and aristocratical party...whose avowed object is to draw over us the substance, as they have already done the forms of the British government." The letter spoke also of the "apostates who have gone over to these heresies, men who were Sampsons in the field and Solomons in the counsil, but who have had their heads shorn by the harlot England." Jefferson had never intended the letter to be made public, and he suffered a good deal from its constant use against him. Yet, for one letter that found its way into print there were hundreds that did not—more moderate in tone but with the same basic political purpose, to cast the enemy camp in the role of reactionaries and counterrevolutionaries.

It was not an easy context within which to work politically. The cause of the pro-French group was badly hurt by the overzealous activities of the new French envoy to the United States, Edmond Charles Genet, who saw himself as a messenger sent to awaken the revolutionary energies of the American people, despite their government. For a time Jefferson had some hopes that Genet could create a new and favorable climate of opinion in the United States, and the ardor of the crowds that greeted him seemed to bear out this hope. But Genet's arrogance and his blunders of meddling intervention in the American political struggle defeated his own purposes and left Jefferson sadly disillusioned, until finally—it was one of his last acts as secretary of state—he had to ask for Genet's recall.

Even more serious, under the Adams administration, was the XYZ episode, when the French directory sought to humiliate the American negotiators in Paris by assigning nonentities to talk with them, and by seeking to extort blackmail from the American government as a condition of negotiation. The anti-French feeling that swept through America as a consequence hobbled any effort that Jefferson and his friends might have made to warn American opinion against the dangers of a war with France. During most of the years while Jefferson was a private citizen at Monticello and later while he was vice president, his political strategy was necessarily a holding operation until the war passions could be calmed. In his public utterances Jefferson showed a great wisdom by refusing to embroil himself in controversies. He was convinced that a hands-off policy would prove the most effective one, and that the "High Federalists" who were pushing Adams toward militant actions should be left to make their inevitable mistakes—which in the end they did.

The remarkable fact about the period from Jefferson's resignation as secretary until his election as president—from 1794 to 1800—was that it was a period darkened by the impact of French Revolutionary excesses upon American opinion, but that the Jeffersonian camp nevertheless came through tolerably in the 1794 congressional elections and got their leader chosen as vice president in 1796 and as president in 1800. That Jefferson was able to achieve such political victories out of such intractable material is testimony not only to his skill of maneuver, but to the subtlety of his political intuitions. There were times when he was tempted, during that dark period, to dismiss the people as "a swinish multitude," but these moments of bitterness were rare. His prevailing mood was that the people could be reached, persuaded, educated; that if they were not always swayed by reason, they were at least capable of reason; that while the political climate might be unfavorable for stretches of time, the tides of the future had set in strongly for the world revolutionary cause. In short, he found himself triumphantly vindicated in his conviction that "the rising generation is all Republican."

I am suggesting that the strength of Jefferson's confrontation of the revolutionary events in France lay in his skill in political warfare, and in his sensitivity to the nuances of popular opinion. It did not lie in any sharpness of analysis or depth of insight into the process of political revolution. In his attitude toward revolution Jefferson was in the advance guard of his time as an ideologist. He was attuned to the winds of change both in the Europe and America of his time. He was sensitive to the aspirations of the intellectuals on both continents as he was to those of the underlying population who had no chance to articulate their aspirations. The combination of his political sensitivity and his gift for phrase made him one of the great world figures: he was at once a symbol of the revolutionary turmoil of his time, and an ideologist in expressing what so many were unable themselves to express. With all his modesty he was not unaware of his own role as revolutionary symbol and carrier. This was why, despite his personal recoil from the reports of the bloodshed in France, he could never bring himself to repudiate in any way the essential direction of the French Revolution. To do so would have been to deny the essence of his own meaning as a leader of American and world revolutionary effort, and his own place in history.

His sharpest failure as a thinker lay in the failure to see that there were two phases—or types—of revolution. One was the constitutional-democratic phase or type, and its best exemplar was the American Revolution. While it had broken the fabric of legality in the revolt against both the British monarchy and Parliament, and by its resort to arms, it broke that fabric only to restore it in the form of an independent republic. The aim of the disorder was always a new form of order; the continuity between the old polity and the new was for a time broken, but never destroyed. The Americans had developed a new principle of democratic egalitarianism on which to build a new society, but they never wholly destroyed the line of continuity that linked them with the European society from which they had come. The very fact that the young Republic was able to hold in suspension both the political strains—of Hamilton, Washington, and Adams, and of Jefferson and Madison— was in itself evidence of the effectiveness with which the innovating and the traditional, the radical and the conservative, could be contained within the new consensus. Whatever the differences between the two strains, even when they called each other "Jacobins" and "Monarchists," each stressed a constitutional consensus.

It is probably idle to ask why Jefferson failed to see what so few of his contemporaries saw—the passage of one revolutionary phase into another as a basic transformation of one type of revolution into another. Jefferson's opponents, notably Alexander Hamilton and John Adams, went to the opposite extreme: because they were so vividly reactive to the excesses of the Reign of Terror, they condemned the whole revolutionary process, and in effect took a counter-revolutionary stance. They were more tough-minded than Jefferson in recognizing the political realities in Paris and the provinces. But like most of the Federalists, these leaders had their own political blinders, and lacked the generosity of opening themselves to the revolution of rising aspirations in Europe. They also lacked the capacity to discriminate between what was democratically valid in the Revolution and what had come to defeat and destroy the original impulse of constitutional democracy.

Clearly Jefferson was more liberal-minded than they in this sense of opening himself to the popular aspirations which the French Revolution expressed; he was also more politically tender minded than they. But perhaps because of this very tendermindedness he gave his contemporaries and succeeding generations the impression of holding fast to his principles, even at the risk of defeat in his own political career. There is little question that he did have this kind of principled political courage which transcended the narrower forms of partisanship and the meaner forms of self-interest, and there is equally little question that he was convinced of the rightness of his principled stand.

But in the light of later world history this aspect of Jefferson as a political thinker has not worn well. He could express universals about the struggle against tyranny and the liberation of the people from the manacles of privilege and superstition, and express them with a felicity of language that makes his letters and state papers intensely quotable. But if we feel that the test of viability in intellectual history is the capacity of the idea to stand up under the pressure of later events, then the history of world revolutions since Jefferson's time has dealt drastically with him.

With all his realism, Jefferson was capable of wishful thinking to make the social reality square with his body of principles. He managed to avert his gaze from the Gorgon-head of the revolutionary dictatorship that emerged in Paris. He continued to speak and think of the revolutionary process in Plutarchian terms as the commitment of patriots to the cause of freedom. "The tree of liberty," he said in his famous sentence, "must always be watered by the blood of patriots." But he failed to ask what cause the patriots were committing themselves to, and what purposes freedom would serve. In the later phase of the French Revolution, the patriots harried political opponents and personal enemies, and freedom was used for setting up a new form of tyranny under the form of Committees of Public Safety. There is a cruel paradox in the natural history of revolutions—that what starts as a revolution of consent may be transformed into a new dictatorship. If Jefferson did not glimpse this paradox, it was partly because it had not become clear enough, but also because he didn't want it to be. To see it with clarity would have been to undercut the sense he had, as an American revolutionary, of being organically linked with the process of revolution abroad.

It would also, of course, have forced him to rebuild his own political position at home, and stripped his emerging party of much of the political and emotional fervor with which it was invested. I am convinced, however, that this was secondary rather than primary in Jefferson's thinking. What was primary was the need to maintain his intellectual integrity, in the sense of the *wholeness* of his thinking. If to preserve this wholeness one had to underplay what was unpleasant in the revolutionary reality in France, then Jefferson had the intellectual will to do it.

In every revolution (including the American) there has been a struggle between the libertarian and the democratic impulse. The libertarian seeks to free people from an undesired authority which subjects them without consent; the democratic seeks to build a new power structure to embody the people's will as the earlier power structure had failed to. But in the course of building it there is always the danger of negating rather than fulfilling the freedom impulse, the principle of opposition and dissent.

In the American case the libertarian aspect of freedom was successfully carried through by the Revolution successfully liberating the people, while the democratic impulse was tolerably organized by the Constitution into a new power structure. But the protection of dissenting thought and opinion was also consolidated both constitutionally in the Bill of Rights, and in practice in the early habits of at least a minimum of respect for the opposition.

Only by analyzing the revolutionary process in this way does Jefferson's crucial role in the American Revolution become clear. As the principal author of the Declaration of Independence, he gave form to the libertarian aspect of freedom; but also, as the principal champion of the necessity of incorporating a Bill of Rights into the Constitution, he gave concreteness to the protection of dissenting thought. His libertarianism as a revolutionary thinker was thus not limited to one of the two aspects of liberty. More than any other revolutionary thinker he encompassed both.

Thus, his failure to integrate both aspects in his attitude toward the French Revolution is all the more remarkable. The French revolutionary activists cared little about protecting the freedom of dissenting thought. Buoyant in their liberation from the tyrannies of the old regime, they stopped at nothing to enthrone the demos. In the name of liberty the people became king; and in the name of the people a succession of leaders fought a bloody intramural battle over the exercise of power, a battle which always moved toward dictatorship. Finally, both liberty and democracy were subordinated to a tyranny of a revolutionary elite speaking in the name of both. That in turn was succeeded by a military leader (Napoleon Bonaparte) whose bid to restore order at the price both of liberty and democracy made "Bonapartism" a generic concept in the history of revolutions.

In responding to this the two American ideological camps almost comically reversed their accustomed rhetoric. The Hamilton-Adams camp, which had little tolerance for the cult of libertarianism in America, and had always emphasized centralized power, found itself opposing the centralized power of the French revolutionary elite, and argued for the protection of individual liberties. The Jeffersonian-Madisonian camp, so fearful of centralized power inside of the United States, found itself defending what was in effect a French dictatorship: the champions of an American Bill of Rights curiously glossed over the violation of individual rights in France, rationalizing it in the name of effective revolutionary government.

Neither camp could have been entirely happy with the intellectual position into which it was thrust. But of the two, the Jeffersonian camp came out of its dilemmas with the greater political profit. The Hamilton-Adams group, which had called for the guarantee of freedom in France, made the mistake of not extending its French position logically into the American context: instead of reaping the benefits of championing libertarianism, it got boxed into a counter-revolutionary position. The Jeffersonian camp managed to gloss over its failure to take a libertarian position on the French Revolution, and emerged within the American context as the sole champions of libertarianism. What counted for the American people was not so much what their leaders said and felt about France, but what they said and did about America.

6

A Party Leader's Path to the Summit, 1789–1800

It is a tribute to Jefferson's skill of maneuver that he managed his ascent, but it was also due to his basic intellectual commitment. His inevitable disenchantment with the course of the French Revolution, which he could not have hidden from himself even when he chose not to parade it before his political opponents, threw him back into a greater concern than ever with the protection of freedoms inside his own country. Put more sharply, it was the libertarian failure of the second phase of the French Revolution which made Jefferson more strongly determined than ever that the American venture should succeed as a constitutional democratic revolution. The new American society had to work. In a letter to General Thaddeus Kosciusko, a Polish patriot who had championed the American revolutionary cause, he speaks of "the loveliness of freedom" in an America that could become "a model for the protection of man in a state of freedom and order." In the mention of "order" one finds here Jefferson's basic concern for an orderly intellectual and social universe, but even more crucially an emphasis on freedom which takes on aesthetic overtones and becomes almost a mystique.

Unlike his conservative contemporaries, Jefferson was not content to make the new society work pragmatically as an effective form of constitutionalism. He was always alert to the danger of having the new republic slip back into a weary replica of the British polity. He wanted it to be a revolutionary amalgam of freedom and order, with a constant renewal of the society by breaking the dead hand of the past, and with a continuing innovative impulse which would keep the revolutionary fervor from becoming stagnant. It was by reasserting this revolutionary democratic imperative, and by adapting it to the changing political configurations of his time, that Jefferson became the symbol of progressive leadership.

What he regarded as the most serious crisis of American freedoms came during the period of war fever in the last years of the century, when astute men in both parties felt certain that war with France could not be avoided. The problem was not one of a clash of interests between the two nations, but one of national image and self-image. The French saw themselves as the current carriers of a revolutionary flame which the Americans had first lit, and they recalled how they had supported the American revolutionaries when hardly anyone else did. They were bitter at the failure of the Americans to respond with similar support for their own revolutionary struggle, as they saw it, with counter-revolutionary forces at home and abroad: they saw the British as symbolizing the counter-revolution at its worst, and they were dismayed that the Americans had ratified a treaty with the British which violated their neutrality. Their way of striking back was to impose humiliation on the American envoys and interfere with American shipping by embargo and by capture at sea. The Americans in turn were affronted by the challenge to their national self-image as an independent republic and as the newest "among the powers of the earth." For a time it looked as if an American effort to break the French blockade and to use armed convoys for American shipping would bring war with it. Certainly the "High Federalists" equated the failure to go along with anti-French militancy with a failure of patriotism, and viewed any identification with the French revolutionary cause as tantamount to high treason.

Not in principle a pacifist, Jefferson was nevertheless deeply convinced that there was no issue at the time to justify American action in starting a war. Even more he was convinced that a war might well destroy the functioning of American freedom at home, and that it would certainly interfere with the strong impulse to carry into concrete institutional life the revolutionary promise of American democracy. Hence, for him the position against the "war party" was also a position in defense both of freedom and of the commitment to democracy at home.

It is a combination that was to recur several times in later generations of American history—that of an antiwar conviction, a radical defense of individual freedoms against the centralized war-making power, and a radical commitment to go on with the unfinished business of American democracy. Where Jefferson left his deepest imprint on succeeding American generations was in this combination of attitudes.

He had occasion to show how viable he could keep it under governmental repression. During the war fever the Federalist administration, in July, 1798, pushed through both houses of Congress a series of legislative measures known as the Alien and Sedition Acts. The most objectionable of them were: an act making it harder for an immigrant to become a naturalized citizen; one giving the president the power to deport aliens regarded as dangerous; and one giving him the power also to start prosecutions against newspapers and other publications for seditious libel against the president and the administration. Together the passage of these acts, and the *grande peur* out of which they came, represented the first of the great hysterias of American history. Comparing it with the post-war hysteria of 1919 and with the McCarthy hysteria of 1947 through 1954, one finds similar basic ingredients: a nativist hostility to foreigners, amounting to a kind of xenophobia; an anti-intellectualist fear of "foreign" ideas and their carriers; a hunt for dangerous thoughts; an equating of liberalism with subversion and of dissenting thought with treasonable utterance. Little wonder that Jefferson saw this whole episode as one of "the reign of witches."

As it turned out, the powers given to the president were used in only a limited way. No aliens were deported. The anti-immigrant feeling was a passing phase. The real clash came on freedom of the press. The Adams administration was rattled and foolish enough to start a number of suits against editors for seditious libel. There was in fact a good deal of irresponsible partisan journalism in both party camps. The more benighted of the Federalist leaders thought that they could check the excesses of the antiadministration papers by legal repression. All they succeeded in doing was to counteract much of the favorable tide which had set in for their party cause after the news of the French revolutionary terror. The political impact of the repressions within America more than balanced out the impact of the repressions in France. In a sense this was the kind of break the Jeffersonian camp had been waiting for, and Jefferson and Madison took full advantage of it. Rash enough to tamper with the fragile structure of American democratic freedoms, the Federalist camp in the end was buried in the rubble of the confusion it caused.

The basic Republican tactic was to pass resolutions in state legislatures, *and* set up Committees of Correspondence in order to take common action and fight out the whole issue on grounds of constitutional principle. The key answer of the Republicans to the repressive acts was embodied in the Kentucky and Virginia Resolutions. Behind the scenes Jefferson was the principal architect of the Kentucky Resolutions as Madison was of the Virginia Resolutions. Of the two, Jefferson's handiwork was the more militant. He took the position that the powers granted to the president and the federal judiciary by the Acts had never explicitly been assigned to them in the Federal Constitution, and that the Acts were therefore unconstitutional. But he also went a good distance beyond that position. At one point, he even dallied with the idea that such a violation of the Constitution gave the people of the various states a natural right of secession from the Union. It was only at Madison's urging that he omitted it from the Kentucky Resolutions. In his own thinking he recast it to mean that such a right of secession existed only in the most extreme cases of constitutional violation.

Deeply troubled by the role which the federal judiciary played, under judges who had been selected largely from the ranks of the Federalists, Jefferson also at one point proposed the popular election of jurors, in what might have turned out to be a species of "people's courts," but this too he omitted from the final draft of the Resolutions. What remained was the contention that the states possessed, along with the federal government, an equal right to interpret the meaning of Constitutional provisions, and that the legislative branch possessed this equal right along with the judiciary. One must remember that he took this position before the doctrine of judicial review had been enunciated in *Marbury* v. *Madison* in 1803, and long before it had crystallized as an accepted Constitutional tradition. He was responding to his own urgent sense of the dangers to American freedom which lay in giving either the federal government or its judicial branch any priority in interpreting the Constitution.

His doctrine of co-equal powers of interpretation, which in one sense anticipated John C. Calhoun's later doctrine of the countervailing ("concurrent") powers of state and federal governments, has not survived in the mainstream of constitutional thought. The states' rights camp embraced its die-hard resistance to legislation and judicial interpretation of civil rights for much of the twentieth century. Were Jefferson confronted with this thinking and its consequences, he could not have possibly accepted this modern successor to the states' rights stand he took in the Kentucky Resolutions. This underscores the need for seeing Jefferson's abstract formulations in the context of the political struggles of his own day. Always strongly responsive to the dangers which he sensed from the reactionary attacks upon freedoms, his flair for putting his response in seductive universal terms often carried him further than he would be willing to go in a changed context.

Frankly and vigorously a party man, Jefferson defended the emerging American party system. While President Washington considered "factions" both dangerous and unnecessary in a democracy, somehow the products of a perverse divisive spirit, Jefferson saw them as an integral part of the process of government. "In every free and deliberating society," he wrote in 1798, "there must, from the nature of man, be opposite parties and violent dissensions and discords; and one of these, for the most part, must prevail over the other for a longer or shorter time." He saw each party as a sentinel watching the actions of the other, and warning the people of possible dangers. Thus, he saw parties as a necessary element in the competition of ideas and programs in a democracy.

In the long run he felt that, whatever distortions might result from partisan demagoguery and corruption, the good judgment of the people would prevail; but that even good judgment could not be exercised without an ideological and organizational core to crystallize the alternatives from which the people could choose. He had only scorn for nonideological party politics, such as he saw in England, where parties were "divided merely by a greediness for office." But, he continued in a letter written at the end of 1795, "where the principal of difference is as substantial and strongly pronounced as between the republicans and the monocrats of our country, I hold it as honorable to take a firm and decided part, and as immoral to pursue a middle line as between the parties of Honest Men and Rogues, into which every country is divided." In the melee of battle in the American context he never had any doubt as to which was the party of honest men and which the party of rogues.

Yet, in his more reflective mood he was willing to grant, as he did in a letter in 1798, that each party could validly claim to embody the republican principle and the principle of federalism. This was a foreshadowing of the notable statement in his first inaugural, "We are all republicans: we are all federalists. If there be any among us who would wish to dissolve this Union, or to change its republican form, let them stand undisturbed as monuments of the safety with which error of opinion may be tolerated where reason is left free to combat it." On the question of what divided the parties ideologically he held shifting views. At one time he thought that one expressed the interests of the executive branch of the government and the other of the legislative; at other times his division ran between Tories and Whigs; at still other times he talked of one as representing the "aristocracy" and the other as representing the "people."

While recognizing the inevitable emergence of a party system, Jefferson in the early years didn't want to identify himself with any party. When he became secretary of state, he saw himself as part of a unified government working with others whose political emphasis might differ from his, but who were equally committed to governmental unity. But increasingly he found this hesitancy about his party role difficult to maintain. The first important break came with the struggle over the public assumption of debts, and it was most clearly expressed in his stand against the constitutionality of the Bank of the United States. It was here that Jefferson identified his party position with the doctrine of the need for an explicit grant of Constitutional powers as against the doctrine of implied powers. In answering President Washington's request for his opinion on the bank, he gibed at the notion that a power not expressly granted in the Constitution could be assigned to the federal government on the vague ground that it was necessary for the "general welfare." What is there, asked Jefferson, which on this basis could *not* be rationalized under the caption of general welfare?

Every successive struggle between the Jeffersonian and Hamiltonian groups led to a further crystallization of their party positions and attitudes, and each new crystallization in turn prepared the ground for the next struggle. But the chief precipitating force was certainly the French Revolution, which forced the two contending camps into positions that, in turn, influenced their attitudes on almost every other issue.

It was not until the election of 1796, when Jefferson was chosen vice president, that he was willing quite clearly to assume the role of party leader. The election itself did not split sharply on party lines. Adams and Thomas Pinckney were considered, respectively, the presidential and vice presidential candidates of the Federalists, while Jefferson and Aaron Burr were the candidates of the Republicans. But a number of those who voted for Adams voted also for Jefferson—enough of them at any rate to give Jefferson sixty-eight votes to the seventy-one of Adams and the fifty-nine of Pinckney. Jefferson's friends were for a time fearful that he might refuse the vice presidency, but they misjudged him badly. Of the two offices—the presidency and the vice presidency—it was the latter that Jefferson quite genuinely preferred, as he noted in a 1797 letter to Elbridge Gerry: "The second office of the government is honorable and easy, the first is but a splendid misery." He thought this way partly because it would impose less onerous burdens on him, but mainly because it was not his time to be head of state: he wanted the issues between the parties to become clearer than they were. He was astute enough to feel that his time and that of his party had not yet come for assuming the presidency.

One must not overplay this as a form of high mindedness. Adams had scarcely begun to function in office before the Jeffersonian camp began to turn against him and to make life pretty miserable for him. Jefferson had built up a considerable correspondence with local and state leaders while in retirement in Monticello, and he now used the leisure of the vice presidency to consolidate the network of strategic political links with a diverse array of the political elite. He was careful to stay in touch with influential moderates and marginal men, such as Elbridge Gerry, Edward Rutledge, and Thomas Pinckney. He was also careful to build bridges even into enemy territory, like Massachusetts and Connecticut, and to make such alliances as the one with Aaron Burr in New York, which added to the strength of the party cadre in that important state.

He did not himself assume any concrete organizing role in the party. He stayed in constant touch with James Madison and James Monroe as his principal intellectual and political lieutenants. Another and less distinguished assistant was John Beckley, who served as both a reporter of party gossip in Congress and as a kind of party whip. Together this trio of men formed, with Jefferson, the nucleus of a kind of party directorate which held constant consultations and formed high policy by consensus. He took some suggestions from men like John Taylor, who was, however, often too extreme to be included in the high party councils. In Congress itself both Madison and Albert Gallatin transmitted directives and organized party action. In the press Jefferson had men like Philip Freneau and Benjamin Franklin Bache to set the tone for the rest of the party press. He was alert to the importance of pamphleteering, and in at least one case this led him to form a curious connection with James Callender, who turned out to be a scabrous type of scandal monger.

There was never any feeling on Jefferson's part that an intellectual must avoid the dust and blood of battle and keep himself clear of the grimy side of political conflict. He was realist enough to know that if you willed the ends of your philosophy you must also will the means. While he tried to set stern moral standards for himself in the conduct of his own private life, he was well aware of the kinds of things that were being said and done in the name of the party by other men to whom he did not apply the same exacting standards. He knew that there could be no cause, however worthy, whose triumph could be achieved without the cadre of party organization and power. He knew also that it was not enough to plan this on a national scale, but that the network and machinery of party organization had to be duplicated in each of the states as well. More perhaps than to any other man we owe the origins of the American party system, in the large, to Jefferson's combination of the ideological and the organizational.

He also understood the economic and class base of party differences. Arrayed against the Jeffersonians was the political elite, which had been in power since the beginning of the new government; the lawyer elite which—more than any other professional group—formed the nucleus of the office-holding class; the clergy (whose conservative bias was taken for granted); and the bankers, businessmen, and commercial groups, who formed a large section of the middle and wealthy classes. Jefferson might make inroads into some of these groups and make converts of particular men among them, but he could hope for little more than a marginal scattering of support there. The class base of his own party lay with the larger landowners, the independent farmers, the middle and upper commercial classes of the southern states whose economic interests were sectional rather than attaching to class, and the newly arising class of artisans and city workers. This does not mean that Jefferson approached party differences primarily from an economic angle: Madison was more adept than he at that kind of analysis. But Jefferson as realist understood that this class base for the party structure did exist, and that it had to be reckoned with.

He was himself the first among equals in the leadership councils of his party, and in time he became the undisputed chief, eliciting a deep respect from his colleagues and something almost approaching reverence from the party rank and file. But always he was the great energizer of the party, infusing it with his own sense of intellectual earnestness and political purpose, smoothing out party quarrels, pushing subordinate issues into the background, bringing into the foreground the elements that could unify the whole camp, putting into highly symbolic terms the ideas that the party could fight for and the intellectual weapons by which it could triumph. It would be hard to find any American leader after Jefferson who was as successful in uniting his party and keeping it united.

He had a shrewd feel also for shaping his public image. One of the things that most infuriated his opponents was the difficulty of combating Jefferson's image as a disinterested philosophic mind, the "pedagogue," the man who appeared before the public as "a quiet, modest retiring philosopher" (the words were Hamilton's, writing an assault on Jefferson in 1792 under the pseudonym Catullus). It was hard to grapple with such an image and hard to destroy the man behind it. The Hamiltonians felt that at any cost the mask would have to be stripped away from the man, and they were furious when their unmasking seemed to strengthen the image of a philosopher reluctant to leave his Monticello retreat, who preferred its serenity to the turmoil of politics.

A good deal of it, of course, was quite deliberately assumed for political effects. Nor was Jefferson quite as innocent of the charges of being an intriguer behind the scenes as he would like to be considered, or might have felt in his own mind. In time, especially after the publication of his letter to Philip Mazzei, the Federalist press found him a reachable target. "I have been for some time," he wrote in 1798, "used as the property of the newspapers, a fair mark for every man's dirt." The assaults on him reached a violence which made his continued defense of press freedom a considerable act of will. Yet in the end he came out of the battle of political images more successfully than anyone could have predicted. He had survived the personal struggle with Hamilton, the battle of assumption and the debt, the French Revolution and its excesses, the struggle for neutrality in the European wars, the hysteria of the repressive Alien and Sedition laws, the conflict over constitutional interpretation. Even in the darkest period he never lost his confidence that the longer tides were favorable to the Republican cause.

In the election of 1800 this confidence was vindicated. The blunders of the Adams administration, and splits inside the Federalist party— between Adams and the high Federalists, and between Adams and the Hamilton group—made the Federalist defeat all but certain. What was unexpected was not the victory of the Republicans, but the tie vote between Jefferson and Burr. Because of delays in getting the election returns, it was not until near the close of December, 1800 that the tie became known. By Constitutional provision the decision was left to the House of Representatives. It had been clearly understood that the electors who voted for Jefferson and Burr had meant Jefferson to be president. Burr refused, however, to abide by this assumption, and contested the election in the House. The Federalists themselves could not quite contemplate the prospect of Burr in the presidency, and they threw enough of their own votes to Jefferson to make his election certain.

It had been a long and strenuous road from the time when Jefferson returned from his diplomatic mission in France to the time when he became Chief-of-State, beginning in 1801. But there were few, even among Jefferson's opponents, who could deny the mastery he had shown, both as intellectual symbol and as party leader. The question now was how, as Chief-of-State, he would translate into concrete action the goals for which he had fought.

7

Jefferson in Power: The "Jeffersonian Revolution" and the Presidency, 1801–1805

What manner of man was it who became Chief-of-State on 4 March 1801? In appearance he was a tall, freckled, red-headed planter with a loose-jointed figure, strong but kindly features, and an air of gentleness that belied the sharpness of purpose and will behind it. He was a man of paradoxes, all compact of contradictions.

He was at once slightly awkward, yet immensely ingratiating; a man of the world who had traveled widely, had seen cities and men, knew foods and wines, yet insisted on a severe republican simplicity in every setting, including the diplomatic etiquette in what came to be known as "Mr. Jefferson's Court"; a radical democrat who was also one of the planter elite of the South; one of the great intellectuals of his time who was a hardened practicing politician, with a genius for political propaganda; a man of intense privacy who loved his Monticello acres and continued to keep his garden book meticulously, yet had more surely made his image familiar and popular than anyone since Washington; partial to attractive women, with a gift for intense friendships with them as well as for casual gallantry, yet a man who had not remarried, leaving the White House without an official hostess; a shy man who never forced the conversation and who spoke in a relaxed anecdotal way, yet was always the center of attention in any gathering; a leader committed to principles, who in practice felt free to abandon them in the service of the national interest; a philosopher who prided himself on the plants he imported, worked in his brick factory, and was an incorrigible gadgeteer; a man of sweeping intellectual horizons with a capacity for minute detail; a true believer in global revolution who built a little universe of serene orderliness around him; an internationalist who presided over the intensification of the American national consciousness; a man who deflated the need for political power and played down the power role of the government, yet who—more than any president before or after him—extended the sway of the American empire.

Yet, paradoxes and all, this was a whole man. Not in the sense that George Washington was a whole man, for it would be hard to match the first president's evenness of grain and the way in which the solid blocks of his personality fitted together with an awesome singleness of impact. Jefferson's was a more complex wholeness, but it was there. He was able to hold in suspension qualities which balanced each other and, by interlocking, gave a dimension of subtlety and surprise to the whole.

As this is written, no psycho-biographer has yet approached Jefferson in detail and depth, to lay bare not only his career line, but his line of personality development and the points in his life at which his crises of identity were sharpest. My own guess is that his tenure as governor of Virginia during the Revolution was one such crisis, his wife's death another, his "head and heart" affair in Paris still another. Perhaps his effort to come to terms with himself on the French Revolution was a political and intellectual ordeal that amounted to a moral one and became a personality crisis of a kind. This has of course been true of every president who has led a stormy life. Jefferson's life was full of continuous strain and tension, even when he was in the seclusion of his estate. His self-contained appearance and the outward restraint and polish of his demeanor may well have kept from view a considerable inner turmoil—as one might guess from his long history of migraine headaches, some of which incapacitated him for work of any kind for weeks at a time.

When Jefferson came to the presidency, he was brought there on the crest of the first popular revolutionary wave since the beginning of the republic. What sort of revolution was the "Revolution of 1800"? Clearly it was not what its fearful opponents thought it would be. Jefferson was neither a Robespierre nor a Napoleon, although his enemies tried to link him with both. He had no intention of lopping off heads, setting up a personal dictatorship, instituting a Reign of Terror, expropriating property—or even of so mild a revolutionary measure as sending all the Federalist office-holders packing. If anyone thought that he would carry through an American replica of the French Revolution, the event quickly disproved it. His First Inaugural was a masterpiece of conciliation, offering an olive branch to the Federalists, setting forth a modest and moderate governmental program, and obviously meant to quiet the fears of fearful men. Jefferson's program, as he was to emphasize repeatedly, was one of peace, a frugal administration, a drastic reduction of the national debt, a lightening of the tax burden, a strict construction of the presidential and federal power, and a close harmony between the Executive and the Congressional majority.

Even the purge of Federalist officials, for which the power-hungry Jeffersonians clamored, was carried out slowly, incompletely, and with little rancor. It should be noted about the Jeffersonian revolution that Jefferson was the first of the American presidents to use political patronage as a scrupulous but deliberate instrument of party power. He had ample provocation to organize a purge of Federalist office holders, since after the first cabinet neither Washington nor Adams had knowingly appointed any anti-Federalists to governmental posts. Yet, his only harshness was to get rid of the Federalists who were either hacks, had talked too aggressively as partisans, or had thrown their weight around in office. He replaced them by his own party faithful, held on to the abler and more indispensable Federalists, filled the new posts with Republicans, and somehow managed to restore the balance between the two parties within the administrative elite.

Yet, beyond this there were three other crucial components of the Jeffersonian revolution. First, the Federalist idea that government belonged to those whom Fisher Ames called "the wise, the rich and the good" was replaced by the idea that government belonged to the people, that if they organized effectively they could wrest the power from the few who had arrogated it to themselves and were using it for their own commercial, financial, and sectional interests; and that nothing—not even legislation harshly repressive of freedom—could arrest this progress of the people to power. Thus, the first element of the Revolution of 1800 was the idea of the power of the majority as an irresistible force in displacing the vested interests of the traditional power minorities.

The second element lay in the alliance between the common man and the intellectuals (writers, scientists, liberal planters, printers and pamphleteers, and even a few lawyers) who were his spokesmen and champions. Jefferson was the first American leader to forge the crucial link between these two groups. One may draw a historical line from him that would run through Andrew Jackson, Woodrow Wilson, and Franklin Roosevelt to John F. Kennedy. With the exception of Jackson, all of them were aristocrats or intellectuals who placed themselves at the head of the agrarian and urban masses: Jackson was a man of the people, but a very uncommon one who had learned the art of imperious command in the military elite, and had become a hero symbol for the new majority. All of them also had a skilled way with political concepts, and could thus achieve a fusion between the idea of majority power and the power of the idea, whether of majority democracy or of dissenting freedom.

Jefferson's was thus the first of a succession of revolutions in American history which were based on an effective alliance between the demos and the leverage elites, whether of intellectuals or of political organizers and professionals. Jefferson knew how to use the mass of the people as his main line of defense, to fall back upon whenever the going was difficult; and he used the leverage elites as his main line of attack against the enemy camp. Since he was himself a member of both elites—the intellectuals and the political organizers—he could exercise leadership over both groups. The fact that he was himself not a man of the people, but a landed aristocrat, did not hurt him as a revolutionary leader. If anything, as has so often happened in passionate political movements, it may have given him a charismatic appeal for the mass of people, by providing the necessary sense of distance between leader and followers.

The third element of the Revolution of 1800 lay in an early version of the doctrine of Manifest Destiny. It was embodied in Jefferson's decision on the Louisiana Purchase. Surprisingly, Jefferson broke through his constitutional scruples, his passion for economy, and his emphasis upon a small and compassable agrarian society, in order to buy an empire at a single stroke, for what was at the time a substantial sum. Yet it was the most important act of Jefferson's presidential career, and a curiously fitting act for one who had come into the presidency as the leader of a revolutionary movement.

It was Jefferson's fate to act out the whole of his career in the presidency against the background of swirling struggle between the great European powers—a struggle which swept him into positions not of his own making, presented him with choices not to his liking, and finally proved the undoing of much of what he had tried to accomplish. Napoleon, who was restlessly seeking new areas where he could extend his empire and hit at his European enemies, got the idea that the American seas and continent would be exactly such an area. This involved the pacification of the French possessions in the Caribbean, so he sent an expedition to Santo Domingo. It involved also a "Grand Plan" to take possession of the Mississippi Valley westward and build a new empire there: he was able to force a declining Spanish monarch to cede the territory to him. He dreamt of the blow that his emerging power in the New World would mean to his British enemies.

The news of Napoleon's design alarmed the American farmers and merchants who had planted their crops on the frontier and used the Mississippi as the only economic way to get their agricultural produce to market, via New Orleans as a trans-shipment point. To see a feeble Spanish power replaced by a potentially strong French power was an alarming prospect. Even more alarming, if Napoleon should be defeated by the British in Europe, was the prospect that the British would come back as a New World power. There were insistent pressures upon Jefferson from the new states—from Kentucky and Tennessee, from Ohio just emerging as a state, and from the areas farther West. To keep the war feeling from building up, Jefferson decided to negotiate for the purchase of New Orleans and part of Florida from the French. But by the time his special envoy, James Monroe, had reached Paris, the French forces had been beaten in Santo Domingo, and Napoleon swiftly shifted his grand strategy. He decided that his venture in the New World would be too costly, especially since he did not have the sea power to carry it through against British intervention. When Edward Livingston, the resident American minister in Paris, broached the purchase of New Orleans and Florida, Talleyrand offered the whole of the Louisiana Territory; Livingston—stunned for a moment—accepted, and Monroe on his arrival confirmed the purchase.

Jefferson was staggered by the chance the new nation had—sudden and immense—to extend its domain beyond any dream hitherto. The purchase sum—fifteen million dollars—meant increasing the debt, which Albert Gallatin had managed to whittle down. Even more, the Purchase meant assuming a power which the president did not explicitly possess under the Constitution. At first Jefferson thought of submitting a new constitutional amendment to give the president this power beyond any doubt, but speed was essential. In the end he rationalized the purchase by saying that it was in the interests of the people, and that the decision was one they would have agreed to, could they have passed upon it.

It was, of course, a case of following what was later called America's "Manifest Destiny" in reaching to its natural boundaries. In one sense it was a curious event—a vast expanse of territory being sold by a European power that had not taken much possession of it, had only an imperfect title to it, and did not in reality own it, to a New World power that had no claim on the land except one of contiguity, and the fact that a number of land-hungry, adventurous, and profit-seeking American farmers had already pushed their way into it. Yet, curious or not, legally valid or not, and manifestly destined or not, it was a turning point in Jefferson's own political thought and action, and in American history as well.

It was the greatest single geopolitical event of that history since the discovery of America. It gave the American people the earth base itself for settlement and expansion during decades still to come. It was a flaring imaginative act on Jefferson's part, which in turn was met by an imaginative response of the people. It laid the basis for the building of what was to become an American *imperium,* in the sense of a structure of agricultural and manufacturing power. By compelling Jefferson to find some sort of rationale for his act in the treaty-making power of the president, it helped make the Constitution into a living instrument for an expanding nation.

Finally, the new territory transformed the future of the national party system. Jefferson had built the new Republican party organization skillfully, had waged political warfare against the Federalists brilliantly, and had routed the Federalists. Yet it remained true that the Republicans were, in 1800, still a sectional party. Their strength lay in the South, along with a few allies of the southern planters and intellectuals. They had no real party base in New England, little in Pennsylvania, and a divided one in New York. If they were to remain an abiding political force they had to become in fact, as well as in claim, a national party. The Louisiana Purchase added new territory out of which seven states were carved, with enough left over to furnish parts of six more. The economic basis of these states was agricultural. Their interest lay in freedom to grow their crops, cheap transport for them, protection against the conflicting commercial interests of the east and north, and the prospect of further expansion westward. There was every prospect that the political complexion of the new states would be not Federalist but Republican, not Tory but Whig, not aristocratic or plutocratic, but democratic.

Long before Frederick Jackson Turner's thesis about the reinvigoration of democracy by the expanding western frontier, Jefferson and the Republicans caught at least a glimpse of how American expansion westward could defeat the aims of the enemy party camp. The impact of the Louisiana Purchase was to upset the existing balance of power between the two major parties, and to broaden the base for the Republicans while it shrank the Federalist base. What Jefferson did, to adapt William Ellery Channing's great phrase from another context, was to raise up a new party world to redress the balance of the old.

In these three elements—the doctrine and practice of majority power, the linkage between the demos and the leverage elites, and the unsettling and rebuilding of the party balance of power through the expansion of American national strength westward—lay the meaning of the Revolution of 1800.

In them also lay Jefferson's greatness as a president. This is not to say that the revolutionary aspect of Jefferson's regime was as dramatic as Andrew Jackson's revolution was to prove several generations later. Jefferson's emphasis as president was not on revolutionary struggle, but on harmony and conciliation. His leadership of his own party was unchallenged as perhaps no other president's has been for a comparable length of time. The smoothness of his relations with the two houses of Congress has also scarcely been paralleled since. He operated through his lieutenants in Congress, marshalled by Albert Gallatin who, as secretary of the treasury, was the most professionally competent man in his cabinet. He also operated through the Republican party caucus, which met, received instructions and proposals, debated them, reached decisions, and then presented a united party front in Congress. The surface of Jefferson's tenure as president, especially his first administration, was deceptively bland and ironic. Yet, behind that surface the active conceptions of party government, of majority rule, and of national power were shaping conceptions of a revolutionary dimension.

How can you explain the contradictions between Jefferson's earlier doctrines and his behavior in the presidential office, especially the gap between his strict constructionist view of the Constitution and his rather high-handed carrying off of the Louisiana Purchase decision? One way has been to say that, whatever Jefferson's own doctrinal views, he expressed the historic class interests of the southern planters and western farmers, and that as a carrier of these interests, he was thus (as Charles Beard has put it) the carrier of an "agricultural imperialism." By this view, Jefferson was scarcely a free agent when he sent Monroe to Paris and accepted the diplomatic deal that his negotiators had made. He was presumably merely a historic instrument for carrying out the interest and destiny of the groups that formed the main constituents of his party. By another view, Jefferson was a man of inconstant purposes and devious means, responding always to the opportunisms of the moment, without any great shaping forces that governed his actions.

I find it hard to go along with either of these approaches. True, Jefferson was rooted in the agricultural class and interest and did orient himself to a considerable extent to its national and worldview. But he was always the leader, never the follower, always the shaper, rarely the conscious instrument. To use a mechanistic economic interpretation as a way of explaining him is to miss what made him tick, both as activist and as thinker. Similarly, the idea of a Jefferson permeable to all the winds of influence around him, porous with the purposes of other men than himself, is alien to the large lines of direction in Jefferson's life, whatever the immediate twists and turns.

In a deep sense Jefferson's career and personality were fulfilled in his first term as president, because it was during that first term—at the height of his mature powers as well as of his political power—that he achieved an effective fusion of thought and action. He had never been a champion of the idea of a "little America." He had envisioned an America which would reach to the fullness of its creative power by building a strong economic base, by achieving political unity and harmony, by maintaining a simplicity of manners and heart despite its rising wealth, and by remaining at peace even in a world of conflicts between the great powers.

It looked for a time as if Jefferson could preside over exactly such an American society. True, the nation had to fight a minor war with the pirates of Tripoli and Morocco, but it was soon settled after an effective display of American naval power. The fact that Jefferson followed up this war episode by reducing the regular navy, both as an act of economy and as a symbolic antimilitarist act, was an indication of how the doctrinaire in him could triumph over the realist. But this was a minor episode, and did not touch the core of Jefferson's conception of his presidential role.

The Louisiana Purchase did. So did the diplomatic maneuvering which Jefferson conducted with calmness and skill. So did his handling of the patronage problem, his use of the party caucus, his relations with Congress, his entrusting of economic policy to Gallatin, and the sense of confidence that he communicated to the new nation as a whole. He was forced into his act of territorial expansion not so much in the sense of bowing to the pressure of the agricultural imperialists, but because it accorded with the conviction he had long cherished. It was the conviction that to survive in a world dominated by ruthless powers, ready to use discriminatory policies against her, America would have to be a relatively self-contained economy. The element of surprise is not to be sought in what Jefferson did but in history itself, which offered him at an unsuspected moment a great navigable stream and a large land empire almost for the asking. Had Jefferson been doctrinaire and tender minded, governing himself by the picture of the world inside his own mind rather than by the operational realities of the actual world, he would have turned a stony face to Talleyrand and Napoleon, and rejected the surprise which history offered him because it ran counter to what he had for years written and argued about the Constitution. What Jefferson actually did showed that he was not tender minded, but tough minded, and that he had enough flexibility of maneuver, amidst his fixity of purpose, to seize the opportunity which might never again be offered.

It is this strain of tough-mindedness which makes many admirers of Jefferson's doctrine uneasy. But it is exactly the working combination of the two—with the doctrine subordinated to the necessary action, and with the action kept within the larger frame of the doctrine—which gives Jefferson his stature. An Alexander Hamilton, had he been in the presidency, would undoubtedly have taken the same action, but within a different frame of values, and with the whole Jeffersonian half of the nation clamoring against him as a usurper of power. Soon after the transaction was completed, Jefferson sent out the Lewis and Clark expedition to explore the Missouri river region and then to the Pacific ocean, in order to map the territory and dramatize its meaning for the national consciousness. Here it was Jefferson the scientist, Jefferson who valued the dimensions of the mind as well as the dimensions of a continent, who took over, and he did so with confidence and skill.

As for the idea that Jefferson's world was that of an arcadian simplicity, a kind of eighteenth-century neat and trim garden amidst the new industrial constructions, that idea too needs qualifying in the light of Jefferson's attitude toward the new territory. His vision remained that of an American arcadia, but of an arcadia which had to be extended westward in order to preserve its character. When Alexis de Tocqueville and Gustave de Beaumont, in 1831, made their trip into the American interior along the Mississippi, they were struck by the principle of egalitarianism at the heart of American democracy. But this had been made possible by giving the American artisan or farmer a chance to leave his settled habitation and find a relation to the soil very different from the trim garden of the developed agrarian society. Thus, even as an expansionist Jefferson did not find it necessary to abandon his dream of an agrarian society, but only to find a larger setting within which the dream could be renewed.

8

Jefferson in Trouble: Conspiracy, Embargo, and Civil Liberties, 1805–1809

In 1804 Jefferson was overwhelmingly re-elected, and took his success as fresh evidence of the people's mandate not only to himself but to his program, his party, and his worldview. In 1805 he began to run into bad trouble with his foreign policy, and from that point on until he relinquished office in 1809 his administration slid downhill, getting into numerous entanglements, stirring up popular discontent and outright hostility. Nothing that Jefferson touched during these years seemed to go well—not the Burr conspiracy and trial, nor the embargo, nor the effort at judicial impeachments, nor his vendetta with the anti-Republican press.

One must cope first with Jefferson's approach to the Burr conspiracy and trial. After his duel with Hamilton, the Republican leadership dropped Aaron Burr as its vice-presidential candidate in 1804, and Burr went off on a wild adventure of seeking to carve—out of part of the Louisiana Territory—an independent republic which would secede from the United States and perhaps even invade Mexico. Grandiose as the scheme seems now, Burr's imagination reveled in it and his persuasive personality brought a number of colorful men into his plot, including adventurers, filibusterers, and soldiers of fortune. What exploded it was not any shrewd intelligence work by Jefferson's officials but the fact that General James Wilkinson, commander of the federal forces in the region and Burr's principal confidant, turned against him and revealed the entire plan. Jefferson reacted strongly and swiftly, placing Burr and a number of his lieutenants under arrest, and bringing them back to Richmond for trial.

No one can doubt that Jefferson did well to take the conspiracy seriously: given the loose communications of the time, and the sprawling

American empire, an independent Louisiana might well have been achieved, and the union stripped of its precious acquisition. But most students of history have been troubled by the passion of his response, and the fact that he took over most of the burden of preparing the case for the government, adding the role of prosecutor to that of president. Burr was probably guilty of having conspired to set up a new state—a purpose that in part was dream, in part a real potential which was being set in motion. But Jefferson insisted upon trying Burr not for his dream of empire and his attempt to fulfill it, but for an act of treason against the United States. The evidence did not warrant it, in spite of Jefferson's strenuous efforts to bolster it and even to influence the composition of the Grand Jury. Chief Justice John Marshall presided over the trial in 1807, and insisted on an exacting definition of treason as involving overt acts, attested by two independent witnesses, of levying war against the United States or having commerce with its enemies. The crucial evidence for this was lacking, Burr was acquitted, and Jefferson's prestige suffered.

The whole Burr episode is another instance of the misdirection of Jefferson's great intelligence and will in a case where he felt that his country was endangered. The vivid sense of the enemy that had made Jefferson so militant a party leader, and had been suspended in his first administration, came back in greater force in the Burr episode. From it he turned, with some bitterness and considerable frustration, to some knotty issues of foreign policy.

In Europe the British and French were pitted against each other in a deadly war of embargoes. The American merchants and ship owners were squeezed from each side—the French seizing the vessel if it had touched at a British port, the British seizing it if it had touched at a continental port. American neutral commerce under these conditions became a dangerous adventure, but an extremely profitable adventure. There was little complaint from the New England shippers. But most of what was sent in the cargoes came from the soil of the New West, whose farmers and growers felt frustrated at the restraints imposed on their products. Jefferson and his secretary of state, James Madison, could well have kept hands off the contending war of blockades while they maintained American neutrality: the New Englanders would have preferred it that way, and a Republican administration was in a better position than any other to survive the complaints of the planting and agricultural class.

This was one issue which called for a laissez-faire policy, but Jefferson decided against it. In some way it became for him a contest of will between America and the two European powers, especially Great Britain, which loomed as the more dangerous of the two because its claims on the American ships and seamen were more sweeping, partly because British naval power was more formidable than the French. One suspects that Jefferson, ever since his days as secretary of state, had been waiting for a chance to test one of his favorite doctrines—that war with its military sanctions was unnecessary, and that the best weapon against a European power lay in the economic sanctions. It marked the triumph of the doctrinaire in Jefferson over the tough-mindedness.

At any rate, this was the means to which Jefferson and his secretary of state, James Madison, decided to resort. They persuaded the party leaders in Congress, which passed an Embargo Act late in December, 1807, which effectively bottled up American shipping in American ports and banned all exports from the United States. As it turned out, the embargo simply didn't work. It couldn't do enough harm to either the French or the British to cause them to change their policies. The only nation it harmed was the United States. Jefferson was operating under the fateful delusion that American trade was a matter of survival to Great Britain and—in more general terms—that the economic nerve was the crucial one in international relations. It was a primitive form of the economic interpretation of politics, and at a moment of crisis for America Jefferson made the blunder of formulating an entire foreign policy around this doctrinaire conviction. The howls from every shipping and manufacturing center were anguished and sustained. Not only did the Federalists make considerable political capital over the embargo, but there was factional trouble even in the paradise of the Republican party.

A more flexible Jefferson, having made his blunder, would have quickly withdrawn from it. But at that point in his life Jefferson could not summon up that much flexibility. He was sure he was right, and the protests from the enemy camp only strengthened his stubbornness. He made the mistake that others have made with rigid policies—the mistake of believing that failure was due not to the policy, but to the opposition against it. Having willed the embargo as an end, he felt bound to will the means for its enforcement. Jefferson had sprung the embargo upon Congress and the people by a *Blitz* tactic. Despite his belief in an educated electorate as the crux of the democratic process, he did little to explain to the people the need for the harsh measures, or consult with them about means of alleviating the resulting distress. When passive resistance developed he chose to regard it as a form of domestic insurrection, and called out the army to enforce the embargo with bayonets. As the resistance mounted, the Republican majority in Congress passed a Force Act, authorizing the seizure of goods suspected to be bound for a foreign port. For fifteen months the embargo madness continued until the addition of Republican disaffection to the Federalist revolt led Jefferson to sign a bill for its repeal on 1 March 1809, three days before his second term ended.

How can anyone explain this protracted blunder, initiated by a mistaken doctrine, resting on a dubious hypothesis, sustained even in failure by a rigid persistence, and backed up by a degree of centralized force which should have been repugnant not only to Jefferson's doctrine but to his personality? One can only suggest that Jefferson had the defects of his virtues, the weaknesses of his strengths. He was not a different man from the one who had seen his party through the difficulties of the French Revolution, had carried on a sustained battle with Hamilton, and had tenaciously resisted the encroachments on freedom by the Sedition Acts of the Federalists. He had a powerful will, not easily diverted from its purpose, nor eroded by adversity. In the opposition, resisting attacks upon freedom of criticism and dissent, he achieved some abiding victories. When he was in power, with the same sense of a champion of the people surrounded by enemies, his strength of will could become an instrument of repression.

But there was one important difference. The Jefferson who had been in opposition met constantly in council with his fellow party leaders and strategists, exchanged letters with them, and was deflected from potential mistakes by this habit of achieving a consensus. Jefferson in power had lost the habit of subjecting his thinking and policies to prior criticism. Given the success of his first term and especially the Louisiana Purchase, he was confident that he could count on his political intuitions. As in his earlier life, he equated his own thinking with the will of the people.

To accept one Jefferson while rejecting the other is too costly a luxury for the historian. Actually, there was only one Jefferson, with a complex personal and intellectual core which resulted in different policies in different situations. The Jefferson of the Louisiana Purchase in his first presidential term and the Jefferson of the Embargo Act in his second term were part of the same phenomenon.

I have spoken of the extreme means Jefferson used to enforce the Embargo Act, and of his willingness to employ a kind of *raison d'état* in the Burr case, allowing considerations of state to outweigh any exacting standards of due process of law. Something of the same kind happened in his attitude toward the journalists and pamphleteers. His lively sense of the enemy convinced him that they were hounding him with a vicious partisan journalism. There is little question that the party press during Jefferson's presidency was pretty wretched. But this applied as much to the favorite administration journalists and pamphleteers as it did to the antiadministration forces. Jefferson as president was a prominent target not only for political, but also personal attacks. His experience with the use made of his letter to Philip Mazzei had left him bitter about the Federalist press. He was further embittered when a gutter journalist, James Calendar, after an unsuccessful effort to blackmail Jefferson, gave to the press the story of an early episode involving Jefferson with Mrs. Betsy Walker, the wife of one of his close friends. Jefferson had his secretary publish a letter with his own version of the episode, unglorious but not nefarious, yet one may guess that it stuck in his mind as an instance of the scabrous methods of his opponents.

The image of Jefferson as a strong libertarian, which has come down almost unimpaired in history, needs some modifying. There were instances in which the Jefferson reality diverged from the Jefferson image. The most serious has to do with the question of a free press. During the Republican resistance to the Sedition Acts a number of Jefferson's contemporaries broke away from the Blackstone doctrine of "prior restraint"—the doctrine that there must be no restraint of speech or press before publication—and developed a new libertarian theory, with an insistence on absolute freedom of political expression. Their prime motivation may have been political: the Jeffersonian minority had to justify its opposition in terms which would protect it not only against prior restraints, but also against prosecution for seditious libel after publication. But whatever the motive, the theory itself of the new libertarianism was, as Leonard Levy puts it in his unsparingly critical study, *Jefferson and Civil Liberties: The Darker Side* (1963), "complex, bold, original, and democratic." One may find its continuation in the constitutional opinions of Justice Hugo Black on the First Amendment.

Jefferson had little role in the formulation of this theory, although his broad generalizations about press freedom, as a famed philosopher of the Enlightenment, did not exclude it. But when he attacked the Sedition Acts concretely, as he did in the Kentucky Resolutions, his emphasis was on states' rights, rather than on absolute freedom of expression. This was also his emphasis in his Second Inaugural.

The basic distinction Jefferson made on the question of a free press was between federal and state prosecutions for seditious libel. He ruled out prosecutions by the federal government, but not by the states—although it is not clear why the suppression of opinion by a state should have a special sanction. In a well-known letter to Governor Thomas McKean of Pennsylvania, after complaining that the Federalist press has pushed "its licentiousness and its lying to such a degree of prostitution as to deprive it of all credit," he continued, "The restraints provided by the laws of the states are sufficient...if applied. And I have therefore long thought that a few prosecutions of the most prominent offenders would have a wholesome effect in restoring the integrity of the presses. Not a general prosecution, for that would look like persecution: but a selected one." There followed a prosecution of an editor in Philadelphia and one in New York and several in New England. They were unsuccessful, and again, with a considerable loss of prestige, Jefferson backed away from an adventure clearly unprofitable both to his administration and his reputation.

In fairness this episode must be seen as only one phase of the larger story of Jefferson's views on the press and—except for these cases—his persistent defense of press freedom. At one point he said, with characteristic hyperbole, "[W]ere it left to me to decide whether we should have a government without newspapers, or newspapers without a government, I should not hesitate a moment to prefer the latter." Between this extreme position and his questionable condoning of the prosecutions for seditious libel, it is good to find him on solid ground in a letter several years before his death, supporting "freedom of the press, subject only to liability for personal injuries." Jefferson here saw press freedom as a "formidable censor of the public functionaries," valuable because it "produces reform peaceably, which must otherwise be done by revolution."

Toward the role of the federal judges Jefferson sustained an early and unfaltering hostility. The fact was that the federal bench consisted of men who had been appointed by Federalist presidents, most of whom had antiadministration political convictions and some of whom did not hesitate to express their bias from the bench. The episode of the creation of the "midnight judges" by Adams and Marshall on 3 March 1801, just before their surrender of power to Jefferson, made him understandably furious, and the Republican majority in the new Congress abolished the circuit courts which an earlier Federalist majority had authorized. When Chief Justice John Marshall wrote the Court's decision in *Marbury* v. *Madison* (1803), Marshall took the occasion to affirm the power of the Supreme Court to review the constitutionality of acts of Congress.

Jefferson took sharp issue with this conception of the judicial power, and never accepted it. In his view, the principal branches of the government had a co-equal power in interpreting the meaning of the Constitution.

The dislike between Jefferson and Marshall, who happened to be distant kinsmen, was both political and personal—and unremitting. As the hero of the XYZ Affair, Marshall had been the symbol of the American reaction against the French revolutionary excesses, which made him a baleful symbol for Jefferson. To Marshall, in turn, Jefferson represented a demagoguery which threatened the stability of property, the rule of law, and the functioning of a federal judiciary. In the Constitutional encounter between the two men, it was Marshall who won, not Jefferson, just as it was Jefferson and not Marshall who won the political battle. The doctrine of judicial review and the independence of the federal judiciary from political control were issues that went far beyond the two men themselves. It was well for later American history that both principles triumphed.

At first Jefferson had wanted to replace the politically overzealous Federalist judges by Republican ones through his power of appointment, but (as he put it in speaking of government officials generally) he found that "few die and none resign." He then turned to a kind of purge, which came to a head in the attempted impeachment of Justice Samuel Chase of the Supreme Court. Chase had said some intemperate and foolish things about Jefferson from the bench, and the charge was malfeasance in office. The House presented the charges, and the Senate sat as a court, with John Randolph—at that time still a political ally of Jefferson—acting as prosecutor. Fortunately both for the judiciary and for Jefferson, Chase was acquitted, and what Samuel E. Morison has called "the high-water mark of Jefferson's radicalism" was reached and passed. No member of the Supreme Court has ever been impeached since, and Jefferson's political attack on the judiciary became a closed chapter.

There is a game that students of American political history often play—that of trying to list American presidents either as "strong" or "weak." If one had to make the choice between the two categories, Jefferson clearly belongs in the first. Yet, it is not an illuminating approach to his conception of the presidency. He was himself a strong personality, with a dogged tenacity of doctrinal conviction and at times with an imperious will. He dominated his administration as he had dominated the Republican party. Yet, while he was a strong man and president, he did not have a strong conception of the presidential power. This is a crucial distinction that has sometimes been ignored.

Before Jefferson came to office, John Marshall had predicted that he would "embody himself in the House of Representatives," that "by weakening the office of president" he would "increase his personal power." Marshall was not far from the truth, although he phrased it in a more hostile way than the event justified. Jefferson governed as president primarily through his domination of the party that had a majority in Congress. Thus, he could afford to "embody himself in the House"—that is to say, use the rhetoric of legislative supremacy—without imperiling his actual control of legislation. Strong presidents since Jefferson's time have tried to use their strength in conflict with the Congressional majorities with a resultant deadlock of governmental powers. No one has ever quite put together again the same combination of elements that entered into Jefferson's conception and execution of the presidential office.

Clearly he did not have Hamilton's approach to the presidency, which emphasized the executive power as dominating the other two branches, and demanded an imaginative and resourceful use of all powers not expressly denied by the Constitution. Some more recent presidents, notably the two Roosevelts, Harry Truman, and Lyndon Johnson, have in that sense belonged to the Hamiltonian model of the presidency. A number of others, notably Dwight Eisenhower, have followed the Madison model, which emphasized a harmony and balance between the departments, and a president who was on the whole self-effacing. The Jeffersonian model, as James MacGregor Burns has pointed out in his *Presidential Government: The Crucible of Leadership* (1966), falls somewhere between these two conceptions. The future may well belong to the Hamiltonian model, because of the crises and complexities which modern democracy must endure. But Jefferson's basic approach, of trying to retain mastery over the legislative process and the larger political decisions through a harmony between the dominant party and the Congress, and between himself and both, is one that will have a continuing relevance even in a crisis era.

9

Twilight of a Life—And A Great Correspondence, 1809–1826

When James Madison was inaugurated as president on 4 March 1809, Jefferson refused to ride in his coach or to take a seat with the distinguished guests in the Congress. "This day," he said, "I return to the people, and my proper seat is among them." A week later he set out for Monticello, riding for days on horseback and for eight hours through a snowstorm, and coming through it well—at almost sixty-six. "I have more confidence in my *vis vitae* than I had before entertained," he wrote Madison. He settled down at Monticello, and never again left Virginia.

For seventeen years he was to live there, in the groves that he loved so well, on his farms, among his books, working in his flower gardens, busy with his brick factory and mill. He played the role of the "hermit" of Monticello: there was a stereotype common to the politician-intellectuals of this era, borrowed perhaps from Seneca and other moralists, which made them lament the burden of public duties and sigh for the contemplative, bucolic life of retirement on their ancestral acres. "Never did a prisoner, released from his chains, (Jefferson had written to P. S. du Pont de Nemours) feel such relief as I shall on shaking off the shackles of power." It was not considered good form to be avid for political office, or even tolerant of it: always the dream and desire of one's heart were to live serenely in the happy valley. Despite the stereotype, one almost believes Jefferson meant it. Certainly he was deeply split between his desire to be a gentleman-farmer-scholar and the tumult in his brain which propelled him to seek a mastery of men and events.

By the time he left the presidency, that tumult had pretty well subsided. The last two years of his tenure, including the Burr trial and the Embargo, had been agonizingly long ones for him, and with his anxieties and rages the migraines came with greater severity. "I have but one hour in the morning," he had written Albert Gallatin, "in which I am capable of thinking, and that is too much crowded with business to give me time to think." Thus, the retirement to Monticello brought a sense of long-awaited release from what had become an intolerable burden.

Even in retirement Jefferson was a world-famous figure, revered by his partisans, and once out of office respected by most of his opponents. Streams of visitors came to Monticello—some merely to see him walk across the lawn, others to visit and talk with him. The estate contained beds for fifty, which were often filled with visiting family members and political dignitaries. Jefferson continued his immense correspondence, receiving something like a thousand letters a year, and answering most of them by hand, using a duplicating pen of his own invention. After his death, his executors found 26,000 letters that he had received, and 16,000 of his replies. His *vis vitae* (or vital force) continued strong, and there were never any signs of senescence in his mind or style. In the twilight of his life he continued to show that to live is to function.

There is a letter of his to his friend Thaddeus Kosciusko describing a typical day early in this period:

> My mornings are devoted to correspondence. From breakfast to dinner, I am in my shops, my garden, or on horseback among my farms; from dinner to dark, I give to society and recreation with my neighbors and friends; and from candle light to early bedtime, I read. ...I talk of ploughs and harrows, of seeding and harvesting, with my neighbors, and of politics too, if they choose, with as little reserve as the rest of my fellow citizens, and feel, at length, the blessing of being free to say and do what I please, without being responsible for it to any mortal.

It is an idyllic picture, perhaps even an almost accurate one.

In discussing Jefferson thus far I have tried to analyze those aspects of his mind and thought which corresponded to the successive phases of his political activity. But in his twilight years his life of action was over and he had the freedom to cultivate all the aspects of his varied interests. One can therefore deal with Jefferson in those years only as a total mind and personality. In a time of multifaceted men, Jefferson was supremely a generalist to whom, as to some of the old classical scholars, nothing human was alien. After decades of controversy about Jefferson as politician and political theorist, more contemporary commentary has tended to put its central emphasis on Jefferson's total humanist culture, both in the variety and breadth of its spread, and the relation of the parts to each other.

A study of his correspondence during these years reveals a breathtaking web of interests: in the sciences, in linguistics, anthropology, archaeology and the study of fossil remains; in the humanities and the classics; in music, architecture, and building; in agriculture and husbandry; in the study of nature as a whole, in the earth and the skies, and the meaning of the cosmos; in the dispersion and variety of the races of mankind, their comparative qualities and their inherent equality; in religion and the problem of religious freedom; in the ways and uses of government; in education; in morals. While no expert in all of these, Jefferson was not a dabbler in any. Whatever realm he ventured into, he probed with a fresh eye and sought to master, and usually he could converse about it with a specialist. In 1797 he had been elected president of the American Philosophical Society, in Philadelphia, and remained in that post while Chief-of-State; when he sought later to resign, his fellows in the Society refused to allow it.

This breadth of cultural interests did not mean that he had abandoned his old love of politics, nor his links with its practice. Toward the end of his second administration a rivalry for succession developed between Madison and Monroe, the latter feeling that Jefferson had treated him badly in failing to back up his recommendations as special envoy to Great Britain before the Embargo. Jefferson finally persuaded Monroe that Madison, as the older and more experienced, had the right to take his turn at the presidency first. The Republican congressional caucus, which had become largely Jefferson's instrument, chose Madison in 1808, and he was reelected in 1812. In 1816 and 1820 it chose Monroe. Thus Jefferson, the founder of the Virginia Dynasty, presided over the tenure of its two succeeding members as well. One should add John Quincy Adams, who had changed his party and allied himself with the Virginia group, and whose ties with Jefferson were strengthened by the renewed friendship (after 1812) between the elder Adams and Jefferson.

The influence that Jefferson exerted over Madison was greater than over Monroe. Madison was a man of intellectual brilliance and power, probably one of the half-dozen best political thinkers that America has produced. Together the two men had formed a historic intellectual and political partnership, catalyzing each other's thought, joining in a common counsel of action which moderated the excesses of each and left an amalgam better than either could have produced alone. But Madison was not Jefferson's match as a party leader or president. In all their relationships the younger man had always been Number Two, never Number One. He lacked Jefferson's force and resoluteness, and as president he found himself turning for advice repeatedly to the older man.

As it turned out it was not in this instance good advice. Having failed in his own program of using economic sanctions short of war, Jefferson on the rebound became something of a warhawk, supporting the attitudes of Henry Clay and the young leaders of the New West, who clamored for a war with Great Britain. Like them, Jefferson felt certain that, while America would suffer in naval warfare with Britain's sea power, it would be far superior on land, and that Canada would fall like ripe fruit to American plucking as soon as the war began. He had imperial dreams not only of the conquest of Canada, but also of either the purchase or conquest of Florida, and the annexation of Cuba. He kept writing to Madison to strengthen his purpose about the war, especially in breaking the resistance of the Federalists to it: "A barrel of tar to each state south of the Potomac will keep all in order. ...To the North, they will give you more trouble. You may there have to apply the tougher drastics... hemp and confiscation." The serene philosopher leading the contemplative life in Monticello still had a hankering for the "shackles of power." The pacifist had become tinged with the spirit of war. The man who, as president, had added Louisiana Territory to the American expanse continued to think imperially. If America could add Canada, Cuba, and Florida, as he hoped, the "empire for liberty" would be grander than when it was first envisaged.

For all his exuberance Jefferson might well pride himself on having contributed greatly to that "empire for liberty." The America in which he had begun to function politically before the Revolution had been a scattering of small colonies along the seaboard, with scant unity, with the beginnings of a passion for freedom, but with little intellectual cement to hold it together and give it a rationale. The America in which he was living, after his presidential tenure, had become almost a continental expanse, with rich resources, a technology ready to exploit them, an impressive mounting population, a strong civic tradition, national parties, and a place in the world consciousness as the symbol of the society of the future. As much as anyone else, Jefferson had helped to make this transformation possible and had given impetus to it. I have quoted passages from his letters to illustrate some of the day-to-day vagaries of his utterance. But the long-range tides in his thinking leveled out the inconsistencies, and were part of similar tides that carried along the history of his time.

The twilight of Jefferson's life was marked by two sequences to which he gave his best latter-day energies. He resumed his friendship with John Adams, and began again in 1812 a sustained correspondence with him which did not end until the death of both men. And he struggled hard to build a new university in Virginia in the ideal image of his mature educational thinking.

The story of the correspondence with Adams contains an element of generosity as well as of drama. Jefferson knew how bruised Adams was after the rough handling that the Jeffersonian forces gave him in the election of 1800. When, more than a decade later, Adams told a friend of both men that "I always loved Jefferson and still love him," Jefferson followed it up warmly; with the help of friendly intermediaries, by New Year's Day, 1812, the long feud was broken. The hundred and sixty letters that followed cover as broad a range of themes, with as much learning and spirit, as will be found in any other correspondence in American literary records.

Despite their fame both men were lonely. They felt somewhat solitary on an American landscape stripped of most of the Revolutionary leaders, with a generation growing up which did not recall exactly how it had been. The bitterness of their political differences was past. They had not seen each other since the beginning of the century, when Adams rode out of office and Jefferson rode in, nor were they to see each other during the fourteen years of their correspondence. Jefferson lived at Monticello, Adams at Quincy, a nine-day journey from Virginia to Massachusetts. They were content to spin the threads of connection with each other through the seemingly unending web of letters, perhaps because each of them could thus round out his career as he had started it, in communion with a revolutionary comrade.

True, their talk in the letters was not only remembrance of things past. It was also reflective, a sequence of little essays on every possible subject by two of the best minds among the little cluster that American history produced before Lincoln. Their busy, darting minds had no inhibitions in their writing, except a gentle concern about being too abrasive of each other's feelings. They no longer had to censor their comments on the chance that something they said might become public and hurt their careers. Ambition was gone, and with it opportunism and convenient political truth. What was left was the ripe fruit of experience and reflection, and the excitement of the prod that each furnished to the mind of the other. "You and I ought not to die," Adams wrote, "before We have explained ourselves to each other." Explain themselves they did, at great length. The result was literary and intellectual history.

If one had to cull the best themes from the rich fare, the choice might fall on freedom, religion, aristocracy, education, and the nature of the political animal.

On freedom the two men reached a rough agreement, although they quarreled again over the Alien and Sedition Acts, and Adams showed less of a tendency toward a dogmatic approach to political liberty than Jefferson did. Their views converged when they wrote of the intolerance of theocracies. Jefferson had fought the clergy and clericalism all his life; Adams, while he had not been as persistently anticlerical, got his fill of the Boston ecclesiastics in his later years. But where Jefferson's emphasis was on the separation of Church and State, that of Adams was on the separation of governmental powers: "Checks and Ballances, Jefferson, however you and your Party may have ridiculed them, are our only Security, for the Progress of Mind, as well as the Security of Body. Every Species of these Christians would persecute Deists, as soon as either Sect would persecute another, if it had unchecked and unbalanced Power."

On religion, Jefferson took his stance on his familiar ground of seeing Christianity as a "natural religion"—that is to say, salvaging the ethical residue of the teachings of Jesus after superstitions, rituals, and clericalism had been stripped away. For Adams this was too simple a view, and he fell back to a critical semantic position: "Will you please to inform me what matter is and what Spirit is? Unless we know the meaning of Words we cannot reason in or about Words." Jefferson answered by citing Socrates and his *daimon*, insisting that the Greek philosopher had not been in "real and familiar converse with a superior and invisible being," but that his own conscience and reason were the stuff of revelation.

On aristocracy Adams pushed the theme which had run through all of his books—that of the natural *aristoi*, which can be separated from the common mass of humanity, and upon whom must devolve the crucial burden of governing men and of sustaining culture. For Adams this concept of a natural aristocracy fitted superbly into his larger intellectual scheme of divided and separate powers resting on the talents of elites rather than on some mystique of the democratic mass. It is striking that Jefferson, the philosopher of the common man, the believer in the ordinary man's capacity to govern himself, found himself agreeing with Adams on the crucial importance of the *aristoi*. There is, Jefferson wrote in one of the classical passages of the letters, "a natural aristocracy among men. The grounds of this are virtue and talents. ... There is also an artificial aristocracy founded on wealth or birth, without either virtue or talents; for with these it would belong to the first class." And he adds that "the form of government is the best which provides the most effectively for a pure selection of these natural *aristoi* into the offices of government."

Where then was the issue joined between Adams and Jefferson? It was on the question of how to weed out the pseudo-*aristoi* from the natural aristocracy. Adams felt that a natural aristocrat was so clearly visible as to be unmistakable, citing the "Five Pillars" of aristocracy as "Beauty, Wealth, Birth, Genius, and Virtues." One must assume that for Adams these did not have to be combined, but that beauty, wealth, and birth were as valid pillars as virtue and genius. Here Jefferson differed from Adams in putting far more emphasis on the differences between the privileged and the natural aristocracies. He was able to push Adams to the wall by insisting that there was only one way—for the practical purposes of government—to distinguish between the two aristocracies: "to leave to the citizens the free election and separation of the *aristoi* from the pseudo-*aristoi*, of the wheat from the chaff."

Adams of course was fearful that this might mean a majority power which would threaten the freedom of the polity, and would provoke the privileged aristocracy to action in behalf of its power. He therefore emphasized again the need for a two-chamber legislative system and a separation of powers. But Jefferson would have none of it. "I think that giving them [the pseudo-*aristoi*] power in order to prevent them from doing mischief is arming them for it." Thus the issue between the two friends was joined, but on a new common ground which neither of them had ever made as clear before—the common ground of the concept of the *aristoi*.

On the theme of the nature of man as a political animal the difference between the two friends was the difference between the thoroughgoing rationalist and the witty, world-weary cynic who had a healthy respect for the irrational elements in man's essential nature. In one exchange they discussed the degeneration of the French Revolution into the phase of terrorism and widespread European war. Jefferson felt, as he did about any event which he could not quite assimilate to his intellectual system, that it represented a lapse from the story of human progress, and a throwback to an earlier stage of tyranny. Adams was of another mind, and he criticized Jefferson's outspoken support of what occurred in France. As Page Smith notes in the second volume of *John Adams* (1966), "Such talk, to Adams, was madness. To applaud bloodshed, violence, and anarchy was to loosen the bonds of society and endanger everything that had been built so laboriously and at such cost."

In this regard, as in others, Jefferson showed one of the blind spots in his thought—his failure to share the tough recognition of the irrational in man's inheritance. He genuinely believed in the irreversible sequence of human progress, in man's perfectibility, and in the solid merit of human institutions—if only the encrusted obstructions presented by superstitions and the vested aristocracies of power and the church could be removed, and if men could be adequately educated to take part in the rule of the majority. When Adams heard of Jefferson's plan for a new university in Virginia, he expressed his skepticism of its success. He saw human irrationalisms embedded more lastingly in social institutions than Jefferson was willing to admit. In a letter written in 1814, Adams told Jefferson:

> I have no doubt that the horrors we have experienced for the last forty years will ultimately terminate in the advancement of civil and religious liberty, and amelioration in the condition of mankind. For I am a believer in the probable improvability and improvement, the ameliorability and amelioration in human affairs; though I never could understand the doctrine of the perfectibility of the human mind. ... Our hopes, however, of sudden tranquillity ought not to be too sanguine. Fanaticism and superstition will still be selfish, subtle, intriguing, and, at times, furious.

10

Reformer, Educator, Humanist:
The Rounding Out of a Mind and Will,
1809–1826

Jefferson's basic optimism was not to be shaken. Perhaps his public life, more successful in its relation to the majority will than that of Adams had been, gave some support to that optimism. Yet in retrospect he must have had some doubts. When he retired from the presidency he could scarcely say that the happy republic of his dreams had been anywhere near achieved. His foreign policy, as embodied in the Embargo, had been a failure. The War of 1812 was to eat up a good deal of what Jefferson and Gallatin had done in reducing the public debt, and laid waste to his dream of peace. His ambition to set in motion the gradual abolition of slavery had made no progress: in fact, Eli Whitney's cotton gin (the product of Jefferson's encouragement of the talents of its inventor) strengthened the economic basis of slavery as an institution, and made gradual emancipation less likely than ever. His hope of merging the Indians into the civilization of the whites by kindness and just treatment, and by training them in the crafts of the larger culture, also proved a failure. His constant appeal to Congress to create a national university had been without result, and Jefferson was dismayed by the lack of any radical and comprehensive plan for the education of both citizenry and elites in a democracy.

What might have subdued a less sanguine temperament left Jefferson undismayed. In the end, however, he subordinated his eagerness for reforms on other issues—that of the Indians and that of slavery—to his major passion, a new and radical reconstruction of education. His weakening on the Indian question came first. He had an intense scientific interest in the Indians, and admired their traits, especially the personal

dignity of their chiefs, with whom he had carried on a long and states-
manlike correspondence while he was president. But he felt that their
tribal predispositions would have to yield to the larger national interest,
especially with the surge of white settlement westward. Jefferson the
continentalist and expansionist triumphed over Jefferson the humanitarian. He still hoped that the Indians could be won over to agriculture,
spinning, and weaving, and that they could be persuaded to exchange
their extensive forests, which were no longer essential to their new way
of life, for new farmlands farther west. But if they resisted this process
of peaceful absorption—as they were doing—Jefferson believed that
the only answer would be force. The streak of ruthlessness in the gentle
philosopher came out whenever there was a clash between his theories
and the necessities of practical politics in the national interest. The be-
nevolent friend of the Indians, and the founder of Indian ethnology,
Jefferson was at the same time a practitioner of *raison d'état* on the
Indian question, and it was in this spirit that he counseled the administrations of the Virginia Dynasty that succeeded his.

There was a similar process of compromise in his approach to Negro
slavery. The dream of gradual abolition ("preparing, under the auspices
of heaven, for a total emancipation... with the consent of the masters,
rather than by their extirpation") had been a genuine one with him. He
had once written in his *Notes on the State of Virginia* that the slavery
institution eroded the moral fiber both of slave holder and slave: "Indeed I tremble for my country when I reflect that God is just; that his
justice cannot sleep forever," and had gone on to speculate on what
might happen at some future date when the relative difference of birth-
rate and other events might produce "an exchange of situation" between
whites and blacks. At times his pessimism about the future was deep:
"Nothing is more certainly written in the Book of Fate," he said, "than
that these people ought to be free; nor is it less certain that the two races,
equally free, cannot live in the same government." But his views not
only on the natural right of the Negro, as a human being, to equal freedom and equal membership in society, but also on the innate qualities of
the Negro, were far in advance of his time. One may find quotations in
his writing which point in the opposite direction, especially the much-
quoted sentence from the *Notes on the State of Virginia,* which he advanced "as a suspicion only... that the blacks, whether originally a
distinct race, or made distinct by time and circumstances, are inferior to

the whites in the endowments both of body and mind." But this represents exception rather than the main drift of his thinking. That main drift was toward what would now be considered a distinctly liberal view, especially since Jefferson was able to distinguish between racial differences on the one hand, and on the other the racial superiority and inferiority which he rejected.

Jefferson's plan had been to abolish slavery by stages, by setting a date after which the children born of slaves parents would be born free, thus cutting away the roots of the tree of slavery, and leaving the branches to wither with time. Yet, the plan had no success, and when one of his young protégés, Edward Coles, challenged him to set a precedent for his followers and admirers by emancipating his slaves, Jefferson had to refuse. One reason was that he was badly in debt because he had been a better manager of the national economy than he was of his own domestic economy, and because his cash crops and other income from his estate could not keep up with the constant improvements that Jefferson was making, and the lavish expenditures to which his style of life had accustomed him. Jefferson's slaves were a necessary part of the security upon which the patience of his creditors rested.

The other, and perhaps more immediately effective reason, was that Jefferson was knee-deep in his project for a new university and other educational reforms in Virginia, and was meeting with massive resistance in the Virginia legislature: to make still more enemies by manumission of his slaves might well have doomed his whole education project, which was dearer to his heart than anything else in his public life. Again the humanitarian, with radically enlightened views, had to give way to the practical reformer who was dependent, for the success of his reforms, on the men who sat in the seats of power and whose vested interests he threatened with some of his ideas. It should be added that Jefferson's act, in his will, of freeing a number of his slaves upon his death, was witness to what he would have wished to do on a larger scale had he been able to do it while alive.

It was Jefferson's scheme for a new system of education in Virginia that formed the main burden of his thinking and striving in his later years. He had cherished the plan for some years, and in 1779 had drawn up a "Bill for the More General Diffusion of Knowledge," with provision for public schooling "without regard to wealth, birth or other accidental condition or circumstance." The state was to be divided into small "wards" of five or six miles square, like the New England townships whose democratic form Jefferson admired; each ward was to have a "free school for reading, writing and common arithmetic"; the best young people from these elementary schools were to be picked annually to get free public education in a district secondary school; and again in turn, the best students from the district schools were to be sent to a state university, where they were to be trained as a democratic elite to counter-balance the pseudo-*aristoi* of the aristocracy of birth, wealth, and paper money.

After his retirement Jefferson added to this earlier scheme for public education a specific and intense interest in a state university for Virginia. When one of his friends, Joseph Cabell, came to him with a plan to reform the College of William and Mary, Jefferson persuaded him to shift his interest away from the Tidewater area of Williamsburg, which seemed to nourish mainly his political enemies, to the Piedmont section, where he had grown up and felt himself at home with its vigorous democratic principles. Cabell entered the Virginia legislature and devoted his life to Jefferson's university project. In 1814, Jefferson had named his new university Central College, formed a Board of Trustees, drummed up support from a number of important names (including President Madison and president-to-be Monroe) and was ready for his long and arduous campaign to turn his dream into actuality. His earlier scheme for public education had been tempered somewhat in the course of the years. He was willing to separate off the "laboring youth," who would get at least three years of primary education at public expense and would then enter their life work as farmers or artisans. But the "learned youth" would go on to the secondary and university schools, and eventually into professional schools. It was for them—the young men who would not be able to train themselves without public aid and an available university—that he was to labor until his death, to provide them with the means for developing their "virtue and talents." He was seventy-one when he set about in earnest on this task, and for the remaining twelve years of his life it was his major preoccupation, even his obsession.

In 1816 Cabell got the legislature to accept a charter for Central College. In 1817 Jefferson found a plot of two hundred acres on the outskirts of Charlottesville, bought it, helped lay it out, and began to draw up plans for the architecture and landscaping, with the help of Benjamin Latrobe, whom he regarded as the leading American architect. By the fall of the same year he completed a new statute on state public education which, in addition to the free public schools, provided for nine colleges and a university. The bill was badly truncated before it was finally enacted. The nine colleges were scrapped and only the University of Virginia survived the legislative ordeal. The lawmakers gave Jefferson $15,000 a year for the university, $45,000 a year for the education of the "laboring youth," provided for a commission to choose a site for the university, and in effect undid what Jefferson had already done in buying the Charlottesville site. There was intensive lobbying by the existing colleges to capture the new university site for themselves. Jefferson, with some of his old organizing energy and political shrewdness, used whatever subscription money he had left and borrowed more in a race against time: his idea was that when the state commission met in August, 1818 to choose a new university site, he would have the buildings at Charlottesville so far advanced toward completion that they would constitute in effect a *fait accompli*. As Karl Shapiro has it in his poem, "Jefferson,"

> You watched the masons through your telescope
> Finish your school of freedom. Death itself
> Stood thoughtful at your bed.

That is how it happened. Jefferson finally had his university, at least in its architectural frame and in the skeletal form of the plan.

He still needed a faculty. He had planned originally to use his scanty funds for only four professors—in the language and humanities, in physics, in the other sciences, and in philosophy, government, political economy, and ethics. But with the new state funds he could be somewhat more ambitious. The new Board of Visitors, which carried over from Jefferson's old Board, appointed him Rector, and Jefferson in turn appointed his first professor, Dr. Thomas Cooper, in natural philosophy. But Cooper was known to be a radical and, in the eyes of some, he was considered even an atheist. The outcry from the clergy eventually forced Jefferson to yield, and the Cooper appointment was recalled. In searching for a core of professors, Jefferson wanted young men with the promise of first-rate ability, who would instill sound republican principles in the youth. He tried to entice a number of brilliant young American scholars to the university, but without success. So the man who had been so much of a cultural patriot now focused his quest on Europe, more as a matter of necessity than of preference.

Jefferson's best chance to get young American scholars was in New England, where he regarded the political climate as unhealthy and anti-Republican, while the European climate, with its strong French intellectual influence, was in Jefferson's view far healthier politically. The New England editors must have had the same suspicion, for when Jefferson finally made his appointments—partly as the result of a scouting tour on which he had sent his young friend Francis Gilmer—their outcry was intense. The opposition to Jefferson's appointments spread to the Virginia state legislature itself, and Jefferson was accused of introducing Jacobin thought and French revolutionary philosophy into the new university. What made him more vulnerable was the fact that his plan had not provided for religious education. This brought on him the thunder of all the Virginia parsons, especially the Presbyterians, who felt that it was final proof that he was building a nest for atheists. It was to little avail that Jefferson pointed out that his plan envisaged separate religious education in a theological seminary. The man who believed in a wall of separation between Church and State could not compromise on that principle, but he suffered in consequence.

He was working against time in order to get his university established and functioning. The irony of it was that this man, who had run a nation, dominated Congress for eight years, all but destroyed the Federalist party, formed a new Republican party, acquired a Western empire for his country, and made every European court react to his views and decisions, now had to beg for a few thousand dollars a year from the state legislators of Virginia, and defend himself from constant guerrilla attack against his choices for the faculty.

After a stormy crossing of the Atlantic the European professors arrived in 1825. The university started with sixty-five students, and professors and students alike were Jefferson's charges as Rector. He was now in his eighties. His health was failing, but he threw his remaining energies into his work. He visited the university every day, riding to it on horseback, walking through the buildings, listening in at the lectures. Even when he was no longer able to do much of anything else, he did the paperwork of his post as Rector and kept his eye on faculty and students alike. Each week he invited a new group of students to dinner, rotating the groups so that he got to know each student personally.

He was not wholly content with the preparation or the quality of the students. They wanted a ten-day holiday during the summer, but the

Rector refused to grant it. On one occasion a number of them drank too much and rioted, doing violence to several of the professors who tried to send them back to their quarters. Jefferson summoned his Board of Visitors, called a student assembly, got the offending rioters to confess their role, and expelled several of them. His liberal theories of education did not include any liberality on the subject of student discipline.

There are several salient aspects of Jefferson's educational theory that need emphasis. The first was his early championship of the cause of public education: it was not until Horace Mann's work, several decades later, that the idea of state responsibility for the education of all received any general acceptance. Second, while Jefferson was willing to agree that most of the "laboring youth" belonged in their vocations, and that only the minimum of public education was required for them, his emphasis was in the other direction: that a number of them possessed the potentials that would take them outside of their class if only they had a chance at higher education. This leads, third, into his theory of a democratic elite which the educational process must produce for leadership in a democracy.

In a later period the Jacksonian concept of education held that no special training was necessary for the arts of government and leadership. In effect it held that a farmer or artisan of intelligence could fill a leadership post as well as any highly educated person. This was not Jefferson's view, and the opposition between the Jeffersonian and Jacksonian approaches is an authentic one. Jefferson started with the conviction that the oligarchies of wealth and privilege were already entrenched, and would overwhelm a democracy like the American one unless a new kind of aristocracy could be developed to counter them. This was the "natural aristocracy" on which he and Adams had corresponded. But he did not trust this natural aristocracy to emerge naturally. It had to be helped to emerge, by a broad-based system of public education which would provide the elements of citizenship for the mass but would also offer a chance for the recognition of unusual talent, and by a structure of free higher education which would give this talent an opportunity to show itself. Largely the history of American educational thought has been dominated by a democratic universalism which was only one aspect of Jefferson's thinking. The idea of a democratic elite did not take root immediately, but took some time to come into its own. It is only in recent decades that there has been a revolt against universalism and toward the kind of democratic elite of which Jefferson was the prophet.

In his educational thinking, as elsewhere, Jefferson had some of the defects of his virtues. Because he was oriented toward the training of a democratic elite, he was also deeply concerned that it should not become infected by the rest of the body politic. At a time when education was largely dominated by theology and theologians, he had the courage to cut the state university loose from these theocratic ties, and to insist upon the wall of separation between church and state. At the same time he was overzealous in his concern for "sound Republican principles" among the instructors of the youth, and he let himself be carried away, on at least one occasion, to the point of rejecting an otherwise brilliant faculty member because of his political views. What this amounts to is that Jefferson cared a good deal about academic freedom from church control, but cared much less about academic freedom from ideological control. It was a mark of the earnestness with which he had conceived of his whole plan that he would not apply to it the broad principles of libertarianism in which, on the whole, he believed.

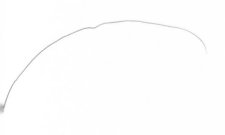

11

Jefferson's Cosmos as a Frame
for His Thought

Jefferson was no atheist. He was not only a deeply religious man, but much of the superstructure of his thinking rested on that fact. He believed that the act of creation had been a single original act, and a complete one. It followed that there had been no later developments to round out the cosmos and that nothing of the original act of creation had ever been lost. Not only does this give a strongly antievolutionary cast to Jefferson's thinking; it also means that in Jefferson's view no species had ever been lost, and no new species had ever been developed.

In the completeness of nature's handiwork, and in its intricacy and perfection, Jefferson found not only one universe, but a myriad of universes contained within that one. His religious sense was his feeling of awe as he viewed nature as a work of art, contrived with total economy and coherence in an unparalleled design by a superb craftsman whom he called God. The perfection of the design was contained not only in the plurality of worlds, but also in an orderly scale of species, from the highest to the lowest, very much like a great chain of being.

Jefferson was intensely interested in this design, but his interest was not that of the geologist or paleontologist. Since the earth and its creatures had no history in any evolutionary sense, but were created by a single act, he could not be either of these in the modern sense. He studied the formations of nature, however, as a key to the larger design, just as he studied fossil remains as a clue not to prehistoric animals, but to existing ones which had grown rare and whose discovery was crucial in supplying the missing links to the chain of being. Thus, Jefferson's work on the "Great-Claw," or Mammoth, was an effort to locate living specimens, whether in America or elsewhere, of a species which had to exist if the chain of being was to be a complete one.

In such an orderly universe the physical regularities were subject to the laws of nature which were the theme of the sciences, and were to be discovered (as I have noted) by careful observation and induction. The laws of society were equally the laws of nature, to be discovered similarly by observation and study. They were not physical laws but moral laws, antecedent to the establishment of society itself, as they were antecedent to all governments and institutions. Since they were part of the original act of creation, it followed that there could be no basic changes in their functioning over the course of time.

In this sense Jefferson's thinking was ahistorical. He did not seek the essence of political institutions by tracing their development and noting how they had come to be what they were. He sought it rather in the inherent design of nature and society which had manifested themselves over time. The truths about man and society were therefore subject to discovery by men. The most profound truths were, as Jefferson noted in his early draft of the Declaration of Independence, "sacred and undeniable," just as man's crucial rights were "inherent and inalienable."

As an anthropologist Jefferson believed that the human species derived from a common origin and was therefore a unity, a single species dispersed over the world since the act of creation. This led him to his basic belief in the equality of man, no matter the race, religion, habitat. Thus, Jefferson's enlightened views on the Negro came directly out of his basic view of the cosmos itself. Yet, while Jefferson saw the unity of mankind as a fact, as an anthropologist he also saw each division of the human species as having found its appropriate home where it had settled, and having adapted itself to the climate and environment with the fitness which characterized the total cosmos. He believed deeply in the influence of Nature as physical environment upon the moral qualities and the psychology of the men who lived where they did.

This is why the believer in the unity of mankind nevertheless felt that the tiller of the fields became a different sort of man from the dweller in the big cities; it was why he was a fierce cultural patriot, believing that the American had been placed where he was in order to fulfill a special destiny in his relation to his environment; it was why he was so loyal and even sentimental a Virginian; and it was why his plan for the gradual emancipation of the slaves envisaged, after liberation, their return to their own African continent where there would again be a fitness of relationship between them and their environment. But it should be added that he also believed in the capacity of the Negro to change his moral and intellectual traits if he were treated differently in the American environment itself: "That a change in the relations in which a man is placed should change his ideas of moral right or wrong, is neither new, nor peculiar to the color of the blacks."

I have said that Jefferson was convinced of the common origin of mankind. But he was also happy, whenever the occasion offered, to have his conviction confirmed. This sheds some light upon the energy which he threw into his linguistic studies. He did not approach them simply as one who wanted to learn as many languages as possible; he was fascinated, rather, by the relation of languages to each other, in language families, as with the speech of the various Indian tribes that he knew, and in the larger relations between language families in Europe and Asia, as well as among the Indians. He was always seeking to establish the relation of various languages to an original center from which they presumably had radiated, which would thereby establish the source of mankind.

Jefferson's views on freedom of the mind were of course central to his whole value system. But they too, in turn, derived from his naturalistic view of the cosmos. "I can conceive thought," he wrote as a materialist, "to be an action of a particular organization of matter formed for that purpose by its creator." And he spoke of "the mode of action called thinking." In seeing thought thus as a form of action Jefferson anticipated both the pragmatism of John Dewey and the vitalism of Henri Bergson. He was himself absorbed with the experimental research of French scholars bearing on the relation between the particular portions of the human anatomy and the action of thinking. While this may seem an extreme form of materialism, locating even the faculty of abstract thought in a tangible physical realm, for Jefferson it was further proof of the fitness of the whole natural scheme, which had articulated even the most immaterial of activities into the world of nature.

Yet, he had a fierce pride about the free functioning of the mental activities which were thus located. "I have sworn," he said in perhaps his most famous statement, "eternal hostility against every form of tyranny over the mind of man." Despite his materialism, Jefferson championed a man's freedom to think in his own way, with his own moral integrity. Unlike modern thinkers, such as Justice Oliver Wendell Holmes, who defended freedom and speech and thought in terms of a "competition of ideas" operating for the health of society, Jefferson did not take so social a view of freedom. He saw a genetic pluralism, a "happy variety of minds," among men as part of the scheme of creation, and he wanted to protect a man's right to preserve his own variety within the larger scheme. He believed that only by preserving this variety of minds could they be given a chance to cooperate in the quest of truth which would be useful for mankind as a whole.

In this valuing of utility we reach one of Jefferson's core positions; he had a horror for all metaphysical systems. While he forced himself to read all through Plato, as a matter of sheer duty and curiosity, he recoiled from the Platonic system, with its essences and its mystique. The hazy realms of metaphysics, he felt, could always furnish a place where the forces hostile to reason could build their citadel. Most of all he was hostile to the metaphysics of the supernatural and believed in "natural religion." His Christianity—and it must be emphasized that he was a deeply believing Christian—was a diffused Deism which tried to strip away everything except the role of the Creator in the original design of Nature, and the basically pure social and ethical teachings of Jesus. The "Jefferson Bible" contains what he considered the crucial passages expressing these teachings. Their impact on the Christian religion had, he felt, been perverted by the Christian churches. He believed in the benevolence of the creator and the total fitness and interrelatedness of the natural design.

He had little concern for the struggles of conscience, the agonies of doubt, the conflicts within man himself, which mirrored the larger conflicts in the cosmos. For Jefferson religion was not a tortured quest for God, as it has proved to be for some of the later theological thinkers, nor did he worry too much about any existential "courage to be." He did feel a humility and a sense of awe about the immensity and ingenuity of the total universe. But this did not take the form of doubts and self-questionings, nor the form of anxieties over the subtleties of dogma. He was willing to let each religious creed have its own dogma, provided it followed also that moral sense which, as a Deist, he felt to be generic to all systems of dogma. Like the Calvinists, from whom he differed so much in his basic conceptions, he believed that America was Providentially chosen to carry out this moral sense by breaking away from the depravity of Europe and restoring the original moral innocence of mankind. One of his cherished projects, which he never gave up the hope of someday completing, was a comparative analysis of the moral teachings of Jesus with those of Socrates and the other Greek philosophers, as a crowning proof of the essential unity of mankind beyond all its differences.

A good deal has been written about Jefferson as a humanist, in the sense that he was a close student of the classical societies, of their languages, their great books, their view of life. Certainly Jefferson had studied the classics hard while he was a young man, and had carried over the habit of reading the great classical works in their own languages. There was scarcely a day, even when he was most deeply involved in the labors of public office, that he did not snatch some time for his Latin and Greek authors; and when he retired from public life he felt happiest at the prospect of giving to his reading the better part of his day. His reading during these years of retirement ranged through the Greek and Latin historians (Thucydides, Tacitus, Livy), the great Latin letter writers (Pliny, Cicero), the Greek and Latin poets (Theocritus, Pindar, Sappho, Homer, Virgil, Horace, Ovid), the Greek tragedians (Aeschylus, Sophocles, Euripides) and the philosophers (Plato, Epicurus, and the philosophical works of Cicero). Just before his death he was reading Epicurus and Pliny's letters.

This reading was a symbol of his broad humanist outlook: in his day the classics were the only working model that could convey the unity of all knowledge, and the most effective way to grasp that unity was to see the relationship between science, religion, philosophy, literature, politics, history, and education in the classical writers and in their civilizations. In the eighteenth century it was still possible to encompass the total sweep of knowledge. Jefferson has sometimes been described as a Renaissance man, and it is a suggestive label if it is not pushed too hard, since he lacked much of the hedonic quality of Renaissance life and shared none of its amoral outlook. The Renaissance, with its revival of classical learning and of the knowledge of classical civilizations, had an impact on the state building of the fifteenth and sixteenth centuries in Europe. The combination of the classical humanism and political creativeness which the Renaissance revived, along with the scientific discoveries of the seventeenth century and the moral philosophy of the eighteenth century—it was the convergence of these strains that one finds in Jefferson who was the inheritor of the total tradition.

The scale and grandeur of this convergence are sometimes obscured by an earth-creeping utilitarianism which crops up constantly in Jefferson. He was thoroughly pragmatist and activist in every confrontation, whether of science, philosophy, religion, the arts, or government. In fact, he judged government wholly by the uses to which it was put in specific instances, and he judged all governmental forms by the uses to which they could be put. His fear of abstractions, of systems, and of metaphysics reinforced this pragmatic bent.

It has sometimes been thought that Jefferson had too innocent a view of man's inherent goodness and perfectibility, yet to read him thus is to misread him badly. He saw Nature as good, and he saw man as part of the larger design of Nature. Yet, he had considerable skepticism about the traits with which man was imbued. "I do not recollect in all the animal kingdom," he wrote, "a single species but man which is eternally and systematically engaged in the destruction of its own species...the lions and tigers are mere lambs compared with man as a destroyer." Thus, if Jefferson saw man as predator and prey alike, he also saw government as the expression and guide of predation. The European governments he had studied as minister to Paris were simply the natural expression of what happened to political institutions when no one set limits to the exploiters nor prepared the people for a more active role.

Jefferson did not believe that revolutions alone could change social institutions and dissolve exploitation and misery, and he had little faith in institutions as such and even less in man's capacity to transform them. Given so pessimistic a view of man's political nature and his institutions, his recourse was to the laws of society which preceded governmental institutions. What he hoped was that a knowledge of the laws of society could keep man's political nature from becoming too destructive.

His remedies were two: first, to set limits upon the actions and powers of the government; second, to educate man as a member of society, so that he will be able to resist the predator and escape the role of prey. Jefferson did not hold a political theory of laissez-faire. His doctrine—that the government is best which governs least—was not meant to suggest that if governments are left alone, with their power and functions circumscribed, the result will be consistently good. He saw the necessity for the direct intervention by the people in the process of government, not only to narrow its scope, but also to set up positive agencies which would prevent it from becoming a tyranny. It was here that Jefferson collaborated with James Madison in adopting the doctrine of checks and balances to the American situation, and in contriving safeguards for the functioning of every form of freedom of conscience.

The role of education in this scheme is therefore, as I have suggested earlier, primarily a political role. Jefferson felt that the education of the people was crucial if the political elite were not to become wolves fattening on their prey. He had no mystique of the common man which saw him as automatically capable of ruling: he had a very clear sense of the distinction between the *aristoi* and the mass. But he was deeply concerned that the *aristoi* should get their badge of office not by privilege and heredity, but by "virtue and talent"; and he was just as concerned that education should enable the common mass of men to grasp the nature of the political process, to limit the province of government, to set up safeguards against its degeneration into tyranny, and to select representatives who would elevate the whole tone of political life.

But beyond this reliance upon an enlightened body of citizens and voters, it is hard to find in Jefferson any actual theory helpful in setting bounds to tyrannical power. Since he had little interest in political institutions, he could not make much of a contribution to the kind of institutional formulation that would have meaning for the American political scene. His emphasis was essentially a negative one. That is why it has been possible for groups far removed in their basic values from his— state-rights nullifiers, slave-holding southerners, antistatist reactionaries—to claim him as precedent and cult hero.

Given the elaborate structure of Jefferson's naturalist cosmos, his political philosophy added up to rather little in terms of a positive view of the art of government. It is striking that one who was so convinced of the existence of laws in the physical universe and natural laws in the moral universe should have been so uninterested in the positive laws by which men sought to organize order in a society. Jefferson was himself a lawyer and his first introduction to many of the British and classical thinkers had been through the study of the law. Yet he consistently undervalued the role of law in a democracy and especially the role of an independent judiciary in protecting the people against arbitrary political power. His lively sense of how the judiciary had been used in Europe to rationalize and reinforce the power of king, church, and nobles led him to see the American judiciary in the same role, as the natural ally of the monarchical and aristocratic interests. He knew the judges as political men, with partisan views and convictions, and he saw no differences between them and the other political men. He refused therefore to concede, as his dearest enemy John Marshall insisted, that the Constitution as they chose to interpret it, had a sanctity above the Constitution as the president or the Congress chose to interpret it.

In human and common-sense terms he was right, in institutional terms wrong. For, as American experience has proved, a democracy needs a respect for a commanding system of law as a cement against its own disintegrative tendencies, and if such a system is to operate there must somewhere be a tribunal to carry the necessary weight and have the final word in interpreting the meaning of the fundamental law. Jefferson was blinded to this need not only by his sense of how pervasive the partisan spirit was, but by his feeling that there was a law more fundamental even than the "fundamental" law—namely, natural law; and that the meaning of it lay accessible to all, if only they would learn to read it.

Within this framework of natural law Jefferson was an utterly pragmatic liberal who used the test of utility for whatever concrete problems of decision and evaluation he confronted. He had little of Edmund Burke's feeling for tradition—in fact, time seemed to him to be the enemy, and to appeal to what had happened to an institution over time struck him as a betrayal of the needs of the immediate present. In this sense he broke with the French *philosophes,* who professed to learn from history and offered to be judged by posterity: the past spoke to them, and they in turn spoke to the future. But Jefferson insisted that the present owed no debts to the past and could make no claims on the future. Rarely has America had a thinker for whom the generational concept and the generational struggle were so important. He had figured out mathematically that a generational span was eighteen years and eight months, and he felt that each of these generations had the right to start with a clean slate, pry away the dead hand of the past generations, and discover its own best lines of development.

His theory of revolution was therefore not utopian but purgative: revolutions were not intended to create an ideal state or society but to get rid of the obstructions of the past and prevent what had served an earlier generation from hardening into a tyrannical habit which could no longer serve the present one. Thus Jefferson was not only an antihistorical thinker; he was also an antiorganic one. The dead were no longer in existence and had no rights; they were therefore not relevant to the needs of the living. Any idea, like Burke's, of a community with an organic continuity over time was wholly alien to Jefferson. This man who was himself so deeply rooted in his soil, state, nation, family, party, time, refused to allow any idea of rootedness to make its way into his political philosophy unless we assign such an idea to his anticity agrarianism. And if there were no continuities over time, everything became utilitarian and atomistic. A good deal of the character of later American liberalism, in the past seventy-five years certainly, derives from this pre-Jamesian pragmatism and atomism which one finds in Jefferson.

For Jefferson himself, such an approach had the merit of giving flexibility to one whose firm sense of principle might otherwise have turned into being rigidly doctrinaire. In his doctrine Jefferson did not believe in strong presidential power; in pragmatic terms Jefferson proved one of America's strongest presidents, exercising his power not out of principle or precept, but because it was the only way he could shape the kind of administration he had set his heart on. In his doctrines Jefferson believed in a strict construction of the Constitution; in pragmatic terms, as the Louisiana Purchase showed, he was willing to use the Constitution flexibly enough to accommodate an "empire for liberty." In his doctrine Jefferson made an absolute of freedom; in pragmatic terms he set limits to its exercise when he felt that it threatened policies he regarded as crucial.

In his philosophy of personal conduct, as distinguished from his metaphysics, his sense of the cosmos, and his social and political theory, Jefferson was (especially in his later years) closer to Epicurus than to anyone else. Reading Epicurus constantly, Jefferson did not hold the vulgarized view of him that has come down in the usual meaning assigned to the adjective "Epicurean." There was no question here of a crass pursuit of the pleasures of the body. Rather, it was a question of the total harmony of body and mind and spirit, with a resulting serenity and well-being. In that sense Jefferson's interpretation was close to more recent scholarship on the Greek philosopher.

When Jefferson spoke, in the Declaration, of man's natural right to "the pursuit of happiness," he took the accepted eighteenth-century meaning of it and gave it that twist, both of elegance and universality, which was his characteristic signature. What he meant by it was not the pleasure principle, but the principle of well-being for individuals and societies. He meant what we should now call the *expressiveness* of human life, not in the sense of "adjustment" or "fun," but of making a living and a life, of following the bent of one's personality and getting a chance to fulfill one's potential.

He was the more readily an Epicurean because of his scorn for the claims of the past and his lack of obsession about the future: he lived, as an empiricist and utilitarian, very much in the present, stressing the humanist uses of the here and now. He cared very little about the sensual life itself, very much about some of life's graces—decent food, good wines, music, books, and "the well-regulated indulgences of Epicurus." He had always stressed what he called, in an early letter to a young friend, the "virtuous dispositions." "Exercise them," he had written, "whenever an opportunity arises; being assured that they will gain strength by exercise, as a limb of the body does." This puts him clearly with those who have felt—as William James was later to put it—that morality should be built into the personality by daily and habitual exercise.

12

Last Days and Death, 1826

In true Epicureanism there is inherently an element of Stoicism, and Jefferson's circumstances gave him ample chance to exercise that, too. His last years were overshadowed with debts and sickness. He had never been a good estate manager, being far more lavish in his own expenditures than his political philosophy allowed the commonwealth to be, and far readier to incur private debt than he was willing when president to incur public debt. He had stood as security for a kinsman's financial obligation of a considerable sum, which he had later to make good: saddling himself thus with a debt of his own. In the one-crop economy of the large Virginia estates, the low price of tobacco, and the lack of a ready cash market for it could be a crippling thing, as it was for Jefferson. His bent for mechanical experimenting and gadgeteering kept his estates in constant ferment, but the expenses of importing machinery from abroad more than canceled whatever income Jefferson got from his ventures. Jefferson lived in constant anxiety, not about himself, but about the support of his daughter, Martha, and his grandchildren, who would survive him.

To meet at least part of his debt obligation, he sold a ten-thousand-volume library to the national government, which became the nucleus of the present Library of Congress. Given his passion for books (his early library had perished in flames at Shadwell, and he had built another) this was a sacrifice, but one he cheerfully made, keeping only his classical and mathematical volumes. He also wanted to sell his land, but at the going prices it would have meant little, so he hit on the idea of a lottery, with the permission of the state legislature. When word got around that the old man was in such straits, however, a public subscription to help him write off his debt was started in the principal cities of the Union he had helped found and to which, more than any other man, he had given an ideology and a fighting faith. The idea of the subscription, and its results, eased his mind considerably in his very last years, although a large debt remained when he died, and his favorite grandson—Thomas Jefferson Randolph—had to manage the residual estate with great skill, and also had to publish Jefferson's literary remains with considerable urgency in order to pay it off.

After a lifetime of extraordinary health, except for the early migraine headaches, Jefferson's body began to give way to the onslaught of the diseases of old age. The spare frame, which had stood up against the ordeals of his long journeys on horseback, suffered from rheumatic attacks, making his beloved daily riding more difficult. The digestive system that had always been his pride also broke down; at first, Jefferson followed the advice of his doctor and took the sulphurous waters of the Virginia springs, but when the attacks continued he grew convinced that the waters had made him worse rather than better, which only confirmed his skepticism of doctors, almost as deep as his skepticism of clergymen. The attacks weakened him rapidly, but he bore the pain and the debility with stoic fortitude.

His informal grace of life was unflagging, as was his courage. He faced death with serenity, as he looked back on his life with a quiet satisfaction. When Adams had written him some ten years earlier asking, "Would you go back to your Cradle and live over again Your 70 years?" Jefferson answered, "Yea...it is a good world on the whole... it has been framed on a principle of benevolence, and more pleasure than pain dealt out to us. ...My temperament is sanguine. I steer my bark with Hope in the head, leaving Fear astern." And to his question to Adams, "Is death an evil?" his own answer was an emphatic negative. This rationalist who condemned all priestly superstitions left behind a sentimental heirloom to his daughter Martha, with an inscription which showed that he looked forward to a reunion with Martha's dead mother in a life beyond the grave.

His end came on a day and in a manner that has made the death itself seem a symbol of the life. He survived the night of 3 July after a fitful comatose sleep. "Is it the Fourth?" he asked toward midnight, and when he was told—stretching it a little—that it was, he fell into a coma which passed into death a little after noon on 4 July 1826, in his eighty-third year. At his home in Quincy his old friend, John Adams, was also dying, equally bent on lasting until the day of the Declaration. His last concern was about Jefferson, and since the news of Jefferson's death five hours earlier could not yet have reached Quincy, his dying words were reported as being "Thomas Jefferson still..."—and the legend was that he murmured either "lives" or "survives," to end the sentence and his life.

Thus, the two men who had been friends and enemies and friends again in life, who had together been members of the little committee to which the drafting of the Declaration of Independence had been entrusted, who had maintained the great exchange of letters in their declining years, and who—among the other qualities and concerns they had shared—had shared also a tenacious resolve to hold on to life, were joined in death, too. They died on exactly the day of the Declaration, while the nation they had helped to gain independence was celebrating the fiftieth anniversary of that independence.

Jefferson had lost little of his political shrewdness, even during those last few years. "Take care of me when I am dead," he wrote in a letter to James Madison, his disciple and old comrade-at-arms in the great political battles of the 1790s. With the procession of men—former comrades, aspiring young politicos, writers, lawyers, philosophers, historians—who came to visit him at Monticello in the last years, he had been careful to imprint on their ready minds the image of his own view of his role in the American past, and particularly his image of the nature of the contending factions and political philosophies that had been locked in combat.

The man who professed himself so happy at the leaving of active political life was still determined that the activists who would enter the arena after his death should do so with the right kind of understanding of the meaning of the great political battles of which he had been part. Hence, he had gone over the *Anas*—the political journals he had kept, with documentation, in the heat of his political battles—providing "to the whole a calm revisal" in 1818 (a decade after he left the presidency), and leaving them for posthumous publication, probably not unaware of the political furor they would cause. The man who didn't want one generation's dead hand to hang heavily over another generation was not at all disinterested in what future generations would think and make of his work.

"Take care of me when I am dead": actually few political figures in American history could have needed less taking care of than this man, who must have died with the supreme confidence that he had left a heritage that would give posterity as much as it could handle.

13

The Shadow of Jefferson:
Legend, Image, Idea

Jefferson's apotheosis—the sudden rush of feeling about him after his death which made a hero out of him, almost a god—was mainly due to the awe aroused by the extraordinary timing and concurrence of his death along with that of Adams. A people which had always believed in America's mission, and in the constant presence of the guiding Providential hand over the nation's destiny, found in the deaths a striking confirmation of God's design. In the eulogies and the newspaper comments the theme was sounded of a basic harmony at the core of the national experience, to correspond to the harmony of purpose in the two lives and deaths and the larger harmony in Nature itself.

It was flattering to the two men, but just as flattering to the American people themselves. For while they were saying that the manner of the deaths showed the hand of God in the destiny of the young nation, they were also saying that they were the kind of people in whose destiny the Divine hand was likely to intervene. Their feeling for Jefferson, when he died, may have been compounded of admiration, pride, wonder, and perhaps some guilt for having used him so shabbily in his last years and having let him die in poverty. But the more they dwelt on the awesome conjunction of the two deaths, the more pleased they were with themselves: what a very miracle-deserving people this miracle-deserving people must be! And their pleasure with themselves made them the more pleased with Jefferson and Adams.

Of the two it was not Adams, but Jefferson who became a legend and whose image has been remembered ever since. While both men were linked in the memorials, eulogies, and public celebrations, there was from the start little doubt that it was Jefferson who was *primus inter pares*. Both men were equal, but somehow Jefferson was more equal. Not that Adams was the lesser intellect: it would be hard to prove that he was. In fact, at first glance one would say that Jefferson was not the stuff, as Washington and Lincoln were, for a legendary national hero. He had no military glamour, no sharpness and simplicity of outline as a personality. He was complex, elusive, contradictory, ambiguous—and an exasperating intellectual.

Yet, as it turned out, these were the very qualities that the generations succeeding Jefferson's seemed to be seeking. Jefferson was statesman and politician as well as intellectual; he was pragmatist as well as ideologue; he was many-faceted, to match the growing consciousness of America as a noncolonial political and social structure. Above all, his political thinking, for all its militancy, was fluid enough to provide the ambiguities that each camp of political thought required in the successive historic eras to claim Jefferson for its own.

There are few political leaders in American history who have left a legend around their name. Washington did, and there was one point in the 1920s and 1930s when several iconoclasts among the biographers did their best—without much avail—to "debunk" the legend; another was Lincoln. As this is written, it is still too early to know whether John Kennedy has left a legend. Certainly Jefferson belongs with Washington and Lincoln in this respect. But the elements that compose a legend vary in each case. In Washington's it was his father role for the new nation. In Lincoln's it was his martyr fate after having seen the nation successfully through a war of brothers. In Kennedy's case—if the legend should grow and persist—it would also be the martyr element, and the fact of a career cut down in youth.*

In Jefferson's case there was no father or martyr role to capture the imagination, only the dramatic context of the death, so that the burden of the long-term legend making had to fall on the Jeffersonian idea itself. In his fundamental book on the persistence of Jefferson's memory, *The Jefferson Image in the American Mind* (1960), Merrill Peterson has used the concept of "image" to cover Jefferson's "ideas and ideals, poli-

---

* Editor's note: In 1980, Max Lerner published *Ted and the Kennedy Legend: A Study in Character and Destiny* (New York: St. Martin's Press). Although much of the book focuses on Senator Edward M. Kennedy, Lerner devotes several sections to John and Robert Kennedy.

cies and sentiments" as they came to be used in the struggles of political action and belief and of historical scholarship after his death. It is a good concept, especially when the stress is placed (as Peterson does) on the interacting illuminations shed at once on Jefferson's mind and personality and on those who have sought to use and understand them.

When one compares the Jefferson image with that of Washington on the one hand and John Kennedy on the other—with the man who was the father of his country and the man who was one of its young sons— what one misses in both the other men is the sheer weight of the idea, or perhaps better its soaring imaginativeness and its capacity to survive crises. Washington had the weight of character, as Kennedy had grace and promise, but neither had the idea.

One might add Andrew Jackson to this list, because of the mythic quality he had in life as in death, and the responsive chord he struck with the image Americans had of themselves as a frontier people. But Jackson, wonderfully congruent as he was with the mood and mind of his era, was not himself thinker enough to meet the needs of succeeding eras. Unlike Jackson, Jefferson's foe and friend John Adams was an authentic original mind, with analytic power and gift for phrase, but it was a crabbed, gnarled, misanthropic intelligence, which went along with political indecision when Adams was in power. However valuable his insights are for the scholar today, Adams was not a man either for all seasons or even for his own.

As for Lincoln, his role was to restate what was usable in Jefferson's thought in the light of the tragic experience of slavery and a civil war. The two men were poles apart in personality: Jefferson was polished, labyrinthine, cosmopolitan, rationalist, optimist, Utopian, where Lincoln was rugged, self-taught, plebeian, mystical—and tragic. What they had in common was that each came at a crisis moment of national development, one when the democracy was being formed, the other when nation and democracy alike were being split. No wonder one responded with a radical optimism, the other with a radical tragic humanism.

Thus my own stress, in looking back at the history of the Jefferson image, is on the fusion of personality and idea in it, and the extent to which both of them proved useful for the felt needs and urgencies of later ages. Historical memory, like individual memory, operates through residues that have been screened over time. Intellectual history is too often limited to the history of ideas: there is also the history of the uses to which the ideas are put by men seeking to formulate and defend their own positions. But if ideas are to have uses, they must be usable. It was Jefferson's gift to have formulated, more deftly and unforgettably than any other American, the political ideas that generation after generation has found usable.

This was true later, to a degree, of Lincoln in his debates with Stephen A. Douglas, in the Inaugural speeches, the Gettysburg Address, the letter to Greeley, the Emancipation Proclamation. Yet for all of Lincoln's depth and clarity, the fact is that Jefferson came first, preempting the chance to settle the ideological foundation of the new American democracy, able to draw on everything before and around him for the first overall formulation of democratic theory and attitudes for Americans. Adams and Madison were also there, yes, but Adams as a conservative was out of tune with the jaunty sense of progress in his day, while Madison, a cleaner and sharper mind than Jefferson's in many ways, lacked Jefferson's sense of command, and took his leads as the two men worked in harness together. By the time Lincoln came, the crucial elements of democratic theory had been set forth, partly in the context of the Jacksonian debate, partly in the debate over slavery, secession, and union.

To a considerable extent the debaters—on both sides, as it happened—appealed to Jefferson's memory, ideas, and attitudes. Neither was able to use him decisively, because Jefferson's positions—where they were not directly linked with the specific swirling struggles of his own day—had been put in terms too general or ambiguous to be applied to the concrete struggles of another age beyond any doubt and peradventure.

14

Ambiguity and Unity in Jefferson's Thought

Some have called this quality of ambiguity in Jefferson crafty and worse—the deliberate aim of being all things to all men. That is an unjust view. Jefferson knew, of course, that every scrap of his letters was bound to be circulated and might even be published by his enemies, just as he must have suspected that his utterances would in some later day be part of later struggles. He wrote carefully, therefore, usually weighing his words for their impact on friend and foe alike. Yet, he was no double-talker nor weasel-worded. The ambiguities lie in the fact that he contained within himself dialectically both the positive and negative principles of later American national development—both an expanding Populist nationalism and an antistate individualism.

There is no other instance among American political leaders of such a fusion of doctrines which square the circle of political implication, from a Jacobin radical majoritarianism to a doctrine of limited powers, laissez-faire, and anticentralization of authority in any form. That is why Jefferson has been the hero both of the Left and the Right, of the states-rights people and the abolitionists, of the New Deal and the Liberty League. He achieved it because, by being at the very center of the early American development, when the vested economic interests and centralized power were still combined, he declared war on both. In time they were separated, and each of them set up its own camp. Jefferson in his own day was thus able to take a position which encompassed what was to become the radicalism of the two opposing camps. Those who inherited his Populist welfare side crossed over for their weapons, and took over centralized state power and bureaucracy. Those who inherited his intense individualism, his preference for state as against national power, and his doctrine of limited government, crossed over and applied these weapons to the uses of the vested economic interests against which he had done battle.

Thus, while Jefferson was a complex figure, he did not split himself. He was less schizoid than is generally supposed. The Jefferson of his own age made intellectual ends meet not any less successfully than others of his time: it was history that split Jeffersonianism, giving the weapons of one to the doctrines of the other.

This may furnish a key to the paradoxes and contradictions and bizarre reversals of the history of the Jefferson image, which have driven strong men nearly insane in an effort to find a rational pattern in a crazy-quilt of ironic incongruities. If Franklin Roosevelt was a Jeffersonian, how could Al Smith—the Al Smith who came to hate and fight him—also be one? If Claude Bowers was a Jeffersonian, how could Albert Jay Nock be? If Earl Browder was a Jeffersonian, how could John Dos Passos be? If William Faulkner or Robert Penn Warren were Jeffersonians, how could Strom Thurmond be?

The quip, "Every man to his own Jeffersonian," restates the problem, but does not suggest the answer. It lies, rather, in what Reinhold Niebuhr called the "irony of American history," in fact, the irony of all history. What is "ironic" is that we expect the world of ideas to remain static in a transformed world of social and political reality. Jefferson, in fact, might have incurred the same ironic displacement if he were to come to life to see what has happened to his ideas, for Jefferson was both overrationalist and overabsolutist, and believed that true ideas, like true love, should remain forever faithful and forever fixed. But the fact is that ideas are wayward in their loyalties, attaching themselves to those who need them and will maintain and use them, just as the urgencies of change make political camps and social movements highly fickle, and thus willing to support—if not marry—ideas which they might once have scorned. Thus, the history of ideas is not monogamous but polygamous, filled with instances of what is called "mate-switching."

We must also not forget how deeply rooted Jefferson was in his own time, how wedded to his doctrines he was. There was also a true congruence between Jefferson and the rising energies of the nation and, thus, between Jefferson and the people. Why should there not have been? He gave them the feeling of progress and the conviction of historic mission. He gave them a sense of rootedness in the American soil, yet also the heady buoyancy of being part of the great revolutionary world currents. He enabled them to feel part of an inevitably favorable future while rejecting the "dead hand of the past." He gave them the luxury of capturing and holding political power while minimizing the reach of the power that anyone could dare hold. He gave them leadership by one of the most accomplished elites in history while attacking any elite of birth, wealth, or privilege. He gave them the dreams of reason without ignoring the hard practicalities of "the empire for liberty." Above all, he taught them what to hate and whom to fight.

If I stress the last of these it is partly because it has not been sufficiently stressed in the Jefferson literature. It is well known that Jefferson was a great party leader, perhaps the greatest America has had. But we do not take the corollary step of understanding how much of this was based on his lively sense of the enemy, and his capacity to communicate it so effectively to his followers that the young militants of each generation became Jeffersonians, thereby laying the base of support for the Virginia Dynasty, and in the end for the Jacksonian Revolution. It was not that Jefferson was a brilliant party organizer, in the sense in which Martin Van Buren later was, or Mark Hanna. It was, rather, that Jefferson was not content with firing the imagination or capturing the loyalty of someone: he had to keep his loyalty, by a continued imaginative appeal, by giving him the feeling of their being directly linked in a common battle against common adversaries for a common cause.

That may be why no other American leader had written so much of his political thinking in the first-person form, speaking directly to the reader. He did this in the *Anas*—the set of diary notes, political reflections, and thumbnail portraits which he wrote in the midst of "the passions of the time," revised in "calm" in 1818 after his retirement and left to be published after his death. He did it in his brief autobiography and especially in the remarkable series of letters to close friends, acquaintances, and political lieutenants which he used as his principal mode of education, persuasion, and propaganda. With all his elegance of phrase and courtliness of manner Jefferson was a storm-attracting, controversy-provoking figure around whom every political tempest of his time swirled. "He was born to overturn systems and pull down establishments," John Tyler said, and there can be no question that this accomplished system builder was also an accomplished master of party and propaganda. He gave his followers unerring guideposts leading to the recognition of the domestic enemy, and gave them at the same time the sense of a sure path to the heavenly city—if only the enemy could be kept from obstructing it. Thus, if he lunged constantly at the enemy, he also reached for the universal and the affirmative.

Looking back from our vantage point, we can see that Jefferson overplayed the enemy, especially during the entire decade of the 1790s, which contained his role as a party organizer and leader and defined his path to the presidency. Hamilton and the Federalists whom he led were not "monarchists," as Jefferson seemed convinced they were, nor were Hamilton's great "Reports" on fiscal policy the sinister designs Jefferson felt them to be, for the enslavement of the yeomen and artisans by the aristocracy of paper and credit.

It is important to disentangle what was authentic in Jefferson's polemical struggles of that decade from what was an obsessive fantasy world—important because so much of the later revaluation of Jefferson as symbol has foundered exactly on the question of his relation to the power struggles of his day and ours. Louis Hartz has pointed out how difficult it has been to develop a nativist American radicalism, because there was no native American feudalism and aristocracy to overthrow, as there was in Europe. The game of class conflict that Europeans played had to be enacted on a new playing field, under American and not European conditions. But while the name of the game was not the European name, nor the reality either, the emigration from Europe, like the great later waves of 1848 and the turn of the century, brought a metaphysical passion that combined the quest for religious freedom with the quest for social justice. Jefferson had both passions. And since the genuine feudal enemy was not really there, in his America, he had in effect to create him.

One notes how hard he worked at it, turning his former revolutionary allies—including Hamilton and John Adams—into figures of malignancy. It was almost as if he were engaging in a mock war, a shadow play of good and evil. One suspects that if Hamilton and the High Federalists had not been there as symbols of high evil, it would have been necessary for Jefferson to invent them. But similarly, if Jefferson and his anti-Federalist followers had not been there to serve as symbols of a depraved Jacobinism, both in thought and action, it would have been necessary for the Federalists to invent them.

There was demonology on both sides. But it was not all shadow play and fantasy. There were real enough struggles in a real enough political arena, even if the model was distinctly American rather than

European. The American Revolution, like other colonial liberation movements since, presented the British with a united front of class and sectional elements which had formed themselves into a coalition for independence. Jefferson's service in that coalition was as ideologist. The American conservatives, including both the "personality" and "reality" holders (to use Charles Beard's terms for the larger capitalists and the larger landowners) were willing to accept Jefferson's basic draft of the Declaration because it offered the broadest base for the common rhetoric of the coalition and for an appeal to "the opinion of mankind." Jefferson was also able to work for the coalition as a diplomat in Europe because the national interests of the newly liberated people transcended class and sectional lines. While he was in France he was disturbed about the Constitutional Convention because he felt that it might betray the principles his Declaration had announced. In fact, as Staughton Lynd has argued (in his *Class Conflict, Slavery, and the United States Constitution* [1967]), it is a tenable hypothesis that the Constitution was the result of a compromise between the two elite groups of the new society—the emerging capitalist elite and the older landholding elite. Jefferson might have bridled at this compromise had he been at the Convention. His lieutenant, Madison, not only accepted it—but argued in *The Federalist Papers* for its ratification, presumably as a spokesman for the landholding Virginia elite along with Hamilton as the spokesman for the New York fiscal and commercial elite. Jefferson did not share Madison's identification with the compromise, and his libertarianism compelled him to press for a Bill of Rights. Yet on his return from France, and as secretary of state, he remained an uneasy partner in the original coalition which was running the new government under the new Constitution and the father-authority figure of George Washington. His teaming with Hamilton in the first Washington administration was a much more reluctant one than Madison's teaming with him as theorists of the new frame of government.

When Jefferson resigned as secretary of state it was because the original coalition was breaking up. He gave the final fillip to the break-up, and since his political talents were primarily those of an ideologist and a party leader he reverted to his revolutionary image of the war years, and for the king and the British he substituted Hamilton and the Federalists as the enemy. It is idle to quarrel with him for his exaggerations in this campaign. This was his political fighting style, and just as it pushed his opponents into similar excesses—which then could be used to justify his own—it gave his followers a fighting faith as well as an armory of weapons for persuasion and propaganda. In a sense it set the style of American party politics, in the struggles between what may roughly be called the "Populist" forces (Jefferson has been called a "proto-Populist") and the Property forces. There have been four major waves of Populism, in this broad sense, after Jefferson: that of the Jacksonians against the bank interests; that of the abolitionists against the slavery institution; that of the Populists proper, from Ignatius Donnelly through William Jennings Bryan and perhaps Tom Watson and Huey Long; and that of the centralized-power Populists, from Franklin Roosevelt and Harry Truman through the Alabama Populism of Hugo Black and the strangely transformed Texas Populism of Lyndon Johnson.

They have all owed a debt to Jefferson and his image. We now see that the tides of history were with Jefferson, and in his basic optimism he must have felt it as well. But how was he to be certain, amidst the struggles of his own day? The Federalists, who had cashed in on the success of the Revolution and on the energy and stability of the new government, were entrenched in the earth works of power, and it seemed a heartbreaking task to dislodge them. It has always seemed thus to the forces on the Left—whether the New Left or Old Left or Very Old Left—as they have confronted the "Monarchy," the "Octopus," the "Accumulation," the "Money Trust," the "Economic Royalists," the "Establishment," or the "Power Structure." If the young radicals of the 1960s and 1970s were more reluctant to return to Jefferson than the young New Dealers were in Franklin Roosevelt's day, it is largely because the focus of their radical energies shifted from economic reform and reconstruction to the problem of black-white struggles as equated with poverty-affluence struggles.

This was one of the two most vulnerable areas in Jefferson's thinking. For all his enlightenment on the issue of slavery he did not transcend his age on it. He did represent the planter elite of Virginia in his basic political and social positions—the more liberal wing of that elite, to be sure, but still the elite. And because he saw the nation and world through the eyes of a Virginian, fearful of the tyranny of the cities as well as of the new moneyed class, he recast the planter in the image of the small yeoman-planter, and fell short of doing justice either to the potential energies of the repressed slave class or to those of the emerging artisan class. In his states-rights theory also he prepared the way for a defense of the slavery institution that he would have himself recoiled from.

His second vulnerable area was related. He put Big Government and Big Capital together in his mind, and failed to see that their marriage was a temporary one. He could not foresee that Big Government would prove a necessary weapon for curbing and controlling accumulations of power within the society, before it could itself be challenged on the ground of cancerous growth and be contained within manageable confines. Because he was so obsessed with the specter of centralized power he failed in his perspective of an independent judiciary as well. He saw the judges as ordinary fallible men, whom he had known as Federalist partisans, and failed to see that even fallible men could be placed in a judicial role, freed from political pressures and controls, and could achieve at least a degree of detachment in holding the federal system together and protecting the rights of individuals and minorities. This failure of vision is all the more curious because of Jefferson's championing of a Bill of Rights, which could never have become a living reality without an independent judiciary.

Herbert Croly wrote, under the influence of Theodore Roosevelt, of the combination of "Jeffersonian ends and Hamiltonian means." This is an easier fusion to invoke than to achieve in practice. The best criticism of Croly's too facile formula is that you cannot transplant one set of means upon another set of ends, that there is an intertwining of ends and means in the sense that each is part of the other and neither can exist without the other. The problem for the latter-day Jeffersonians—among whom this writer must in candor include himself—has been to find means which are as integral to Jefferson's ends as his own means were in his own day. There will be a good deal of the Hamiltonian in them perhaps, but a good deal more that Hamilton would have resented and fought.

In this end-means continuum one would have to include a number of ideas we associate with Jefferson: a faith in the ordinary man and his capacity to govern himself, a belief in the competition of ideas in the press and other media despite their unavoidable abuses, a conviction about the essential psychological unity of mankind, a skepticism about power in all its forms along with a pragmatic use of power when necessary for necessary ends, an emphasis on the ethos of any polity, a refusal to allow the dead past to tyrannize over the living present, an emphasis on the education of a democratic elite as well as the whole citizenry, a faith in equal access to equal life-chances, a belief that the inner health of a society is its best weapon in whatever political warfare it must wage with others.

Jefferson did not always fulfill what he aimed at in this ends-means continuum. But he came close enough to remain a moving symbol of what it means to be a democrat (with a small d), whatever one's party label, and to be an activist—sometimes a partisan—in pursuit of one's ends. Just as he is probably America's best example of a rounded personality, so he may be counted as having striven for Henri Bergson's injunction to a congress of philosophers: "Act as men of thought, think as men of action." It is the interrelation of thought and action in Jefferson that makes him a curiously compelling and enduring figure.

Appendix:
Jefferson as a Man of Letters

Editor's note: Before deciding to publish a short interpretive study of Thomas Jefferson on its own, Max Lerner worked on a lengthy additional section, "Jefferson's Mind and Faith in His Writings." Lerner selected a diverse array of works to illustrate specific phases of Jefferson's career as a man of letters. Lerner drafted short prefaces to introduce the various types of prose represented. What follows are excerpts from these prefaces, emphasizing Lerner's assessment of Jefferson as a literary stylist, who addressed a wide range of topics in distinctly different ways. This commentary extends and amplifies Lerner's analysis of Jefferson as "a whole man."

The Memoirs

Jefferson's *Autobiography* is not a great work, but it has supplementary illuminations for any biographical sketch. Its easy flow, sometimes unendingly so, shows the mark of an old man of seventy-seven who knew he had only a few more years of life and wanted to leave for posterity an accurate account of himself—at least, as he appeared to himself looking down the corridors of the years.

One remarkable thing about the narrative is that it contains almost nothing of his interior life, but is focused on the struggles, conflicts, achievements, and the external events he witnessed. The man who prided himself on being in the political and scientific vanguard was far behind Rousseau and Laurence Sterne in exploring and revealing the human psyche. Such a literary and psychological radicalism was beyond him. As an American aristocrat of taste and sensitivity, he avoided any narcissist self-absorption.

He also avoided the appearances of the polemical. He resisted the temptation of giving any forceful and biting descriptions of his contemporaries, as other political memoirs have done. Perhaps he felt that the *Anas,* the political diaries of his years as secretary of state, were sufficiently full and mordant on the character of his arch-opponent, Alexander Hamilton, with some remarks also on Washington and his other colleagues, and he could leave it at that in his more mellow years.

One notes also the emphasis and foreshortenings. Jefferson's father is discussed at length, his mother almost not at all; he dwells on his Revolutionary struggles and his legislative achievements in Virginia, but says almost nothing about his tenure as governor, which was scarcely a glorious one. These are some good insights into the theory and dynamics of the American Revolution: Jefferson is aware of the role of the young Virginia vanguard in trying to push their older Establishment colleagues to "the point of forwardness and zeal which the times required." He also sees, as a good propagandist should, the crucial nature of the Committees of Correspondence and the symbolic value of proclaiming a day of fasting. And he gives us an analysis of the political theory of his extraordinary paper, *A Summary View of the Rights of British America,* and of the political logic he used in taking the radical position that "British America" was an equal partner with England under the king—a position that led to the Declaration of Independence. His comments on the presidential tenure were to prove important: he assumed that it was the intent of the framers to give the president two terms (the first "probationary") and to stop after that. His indictment of judges has become classic.

Yet, despite these comments on America, Jefferson reserved his major attention for the events he witnessed in Europe during his years as American emissary, especially a detailed account of the coming of the French Revolution. To the end of his life Jefferson was obsessed, not with the Revolution he helped make and understood pretty well, but with the one he had no hand in making, except for his contacts with the marginal group of liberal aristocrats, whom history quickly bypassed. It was also the one that continued to puzzle him. In his memories at seventy-seven, the Revolution had been almost whittled down to the baleful influence of the queen, Marie Antoinette, whom he sees as wilful, frivolous, pleasure-loving, and the center of a sinister reactionary Court cabal. This personalizing of history seems curious in a man who felt that the forces of history were worldwide.

Jefferson had a chance in his *Autobiography* to assess, on mature reflection, why the American Revolution was consolidated in its Constitutional phase while the French moved into a Reign of Terror and reaction. He didn't grasp it. There is only the plaintive comment that the French Revolution *could have* stopped with a liberal limited monarchy. Throughout his account his belief in the people as a historic force is unwavering. Only at one point does a glimmer of a question arise: "They were unconscious of (for who could foresee?) the melancholy sequel of their well-meant perseverance."

What he doesn't add to his "Who could foresee?" is that crusty John Adams foresaw it, and his arch-enemy, Hamilton. There were many others who foresaw it. But Jefferson, with all his intellectual virtues, had the defects of those virtues, the blinkers of his galloping gait.

Revolutionary Papers

Of the many legislative projects of Jefferson in the revolutionary phase of his life, two bear scrutiny: the bill for establishing religious freedom—because Jefferson himself valued it so highly and because it is central (along with Madison's thinking) in the American tradition of the separating wall between Church and State—and the bill concerning slaves—because the continuing debate over the history of the Negro in America, and over racial integration and separatism, gives it a genuine relevance.

The striking thing about Jefferson's approach to religious freedom was that he saw it as basic, not because of any conception of the fundamental nature of religion, as the *primum mobile* of all striving, but simply as a phase of the larger freedom of the mind. His arguments for religious freedom are all arguments for intellectual freedom, and arise less from a design to give every man the enrichment of his own kind of religious belief than from a conviction that religious fanaticism must be kept from messing up civil society. Jefferson also states here, more forcefully than anywhere else, his belief in the efficacy of the idea "that truth is great and will prevail if left to herself; that she is the proper and sufficient antagonist to error, and has nothing to fear from the conflict." One is reminded of Milton's *Areopagitica*: "Let truth and falsehood grapple: who ever knew Truth put to the worse in a free and open encounter?"

The striking thing about a Bill Concerning Slaves is that Jefferson wanted the slaves protected by law, and he preferred a solution to the slavery problem by the personal freeing (manumission) of slaves, but he didn't want a society in which whites and blacks lived side by side.

He did not believe the races to be unequal in their abilities, but he did believe them incompatible. He therefore wanted the slaves, once freed, to leave Virginia.

Notes on the State of Virginia

Jefferson's *Notes on the State of Virginia* is a book of an almost naive charm and an intense cultural patriotism. No other state can boast an anatomist as distinguished and as dedicated. Written over the course of two years (1781 and 1782), originally for the use of one of Jefferson's friends in Europe, it is at once a lyrical love poem to Virginia and the American earth and also Jefferson's way of coming to terms with the natural environment which was so deeply part of his total moral and political thinking. The book is divided into twenty-three sections, each in answer to a "Query" by the "distinguished Foreigner." From the book, a reader sees the many-faceted structure of Jefferson's thought at a transition moment when the American Revolution was not yet securely won and the French Revolution had not begun.

The book, first of all, celebrates the grandeurs of the Virginia (and by extension the American) landscape. Jefferson must be seen as part of the movement which made the romantic landscape a central part of the vision of human sensibility to natural creation. At one point he describes the passage of the Potomac through the Ridge as "one of the most stupendous scenes in nature"; at another he notes that many Virginians who have lived not far from the Natural Bridge have never seen "these monuments of a war between rivers and mountains, which must have shaken the earth itself to its centre."

His prideful resentment as a Virginian and American was particularly stirred by the writings of a French naturalist, Comte Georges de Buffon, which were condescending not only toward American animal life, but toward the American Indians and toward American talent in general. Jefferson's answer shows the qualities that were to make him a gifted, although still amateur, paleontologist, archaeologist, ethnographer, and student of linguistics. His earnest argument reveals his conception of the cosmos and of an economy of Nature in it, of the great chain of being—existing from the first moment of Creation to the present, with no breaks in the animal links, and no animals extinct, mouse to mammoth.

The relation between men and environment within this cosmological scheme is crucial in Jefferson's book, as it was in all his writings. The chain of being is as God made it, but the size, sturdiness, and quality both of animals and men are derived from the particular natural and social environment; hence, Jefferson's defense of the size of American animals, and his little treatises on Indians and blacks in America. The Indian woman has fewer children because of the Indian ways of war and life, not because of her basic nature. Married to a white, with another way of life, she is as fertile as white women. The American Negro has not been given a chance, because of the slave institution, to develop his potential qualities. Jefferson denies that a black person is inferior to the white in inherent qualities, but insists that his or her traits and capacities are different. But even with manumission Jefferson feels that the Negro will be better off in his native environment of Africa than in Virginia. He was thus what we might call a humanitarian separatist rather than an integrationist. That he was less than egalitarian in his view of Negro capacities is not surprising when one remembers that he was still a Virginia planter and politician, liberal for his day, but with an eye to the sentiment of his fellow Virginians. He was to be plagued for the rest of his life by this ambiguity in his thought and feelings about the Negro.

This ambiguity did not keep Jefferson, in the *Notes,* from celebrating American freedom. One might object that this emphasis on liberty in America seems curious from a man who, in the Declaration, had asserted freedom as a universal natural right. But this would fail to distinguish between the *ought* and the *is,* between the proposition that men have a *natural right* to be free everywhere, and Jefferson's view that they have achieved this freedom in America because of special circumstances in the relation between man and his environment.

But Jefferson as egalitarian believed all his life that freedom, equal opportunity, and the good life could not be fulfilled—even in an America of farmers and small proprietors—without continued struggle.

Letters

Jefferson as letter writer used his letters as a triple instrument—as a way of self-expression and literary release, crucial for a man who was a poor public speaker but a genius with the pen; as a space-binding way of holding his sprawling community of friends together; and as a way of scientific communication and political persuasion. He ranks easily as one of the prolific letter writers of his era, when letters were both an art and a necessity, before our own era in which the necessity has subsided and the art has eroded. He is also one of the great letter writers of American history, ranking with his rival and friend, John Adams, and with Henry Adams and Justice Oliver Wendell Holmes.

His letter-writing style is at its worst when the letters read like public papers, at its best when they are private and earthy. The qualities of his style, along with pungency when he has it, are a courtly grace, an elegance which is rarely obtrusive, an effortless flow, a verbal economy which probes an idea to the bone, with little rhetorical explanation. This quality of spareness is evident in the earliest letter we have of his—to his guardian on his education—and in the down-to-business letters about science, gadgets, and politics. They also show up in his reporter's description of events and people he has observed, as in the letters about the French scene and the French Revolution.

When Jefferson writes about love, as in his early letters on his courtship, and on the little community of the Virginia elite, his letters have a labored and artificial charm. When he turns to Polonius, as he does in his father letters to his daughter and his teacher letters to nephews, cousins, and more distant relations, they have a preachy pedantry from which they are barely rescued by Jefferson's knowledge of the right word even when he is intolerably didactic.

In his letters from 1760 through 1789, there are dreams, passionate curiosity, grave ideas for reform and revolution, notes on inventions and technology, perceptive insights into science, and alertness to whatever he found that was innovative. Above all, there was the capacity for wonder, whether at the beauty of landscape in Virginia or France, or the beauty and grace of the women to whom he found himself drawn.

The foremost of these was, of course, Maria Cosway, a talented painter and a great beauty, with Italian blood and an English husband, with whom Jefferson fell more deeply in love than he had counted on. His famous letter, in the form of "A Dialogue Between my Head and My Heart," is a little masterpiece of eighteenth-century sentiment and sensibility. It is artificial in form, with a language of conventional passion and conventional restraint which are placed in formal opposition to each other as in a ritual duel.

Yet, it manages to convey a depth of emotion that breaks through the neat literary structure and strips Jefferson more nakedly to the bone and marrow of his being than anything he ever wrote. By the side of it his youthful letters about his love for a girl in Williamsburg seem callow. The mature Jefferson, on a kind of moral holiday from his American urgencies in an old European civilization, uses all the forms of the Old World to hide—but not quite hide—the authentic passion of the New World.

There is a hint of the theme of new energy and old forms, innocence and sophistication, that Henry James was later to develop at great length in his novels about American experience with European civilization.

Throughout the "Dialogue" there is an impressive skill in the way Jefferson uses the mock debate to re-traverse in memory his encounters with Maria, dwelling fondly on every detail: his pretense about admiring the architectural beauty around him when it was another beauty that transfixed him, his maneuvers to clear away his other engagements in order to dine with his new friend, his half-mocking defense of American landscape and mores against the European, his dallying with the dream that the lady will come to America and share his friendship and fortunes, his sorrows, and joys.

The literary skills are all there, and they show the author to have been not only a political writer, but in a double sense an authentic man of letters. But Jefferson's virtuosity, and his elaborate parade of conventional honor, must not be allowed to disguise wholly the importance of this episode in his emotional life.

We don't know what may have happened between the American minister and the Italian-English beauty that is not revealed in the letter. There is every indication that Benjamin Franklin, who held the ministerial post before Jefferson, and Gouverneur Morris, who held it later, both enjoyed more than flirtations with the French ladies. Jefferson's parting reference to "My wrist, which mends slowly, and my mind which mends not at all," recalls the episode when he tried to jump a fence while walking along the Seine with his companion, and suggests a not impossible liaison about which it is futile to make any guesses. But the greater probability is that Jefferson maintained his self-restraint more than Franklin and Morris did. He was not Poor Richard, who mocked in his life the Puritanism he celebrated in his writings, nor the New York bourgeois with a wooden leg, who explored the pleasures of Europe. He was

a Virginia aristocrat who didn't have to wreak himself on the Old World
to compensate for the insecurities of the New.

Political Prose

On his return from France one can't help feeling that Jefferson suffered a sea change, as if he had put away the delights of his French days
and had stripped himself down for the battles ahead.

His political diaries—the *Anas*—start at this point in his life, and
while they continue into his presidential years it is at a slower pace, and
most of them refer to events during his fighting years as an embattled
party leader. Jefferson says that he collected the *Anas* for publication as
an answer to John Marshall's distortions, in his *Life of Washington,* to
set the historical record straight. That may have been his conscious and
rationalized motive. But behind it there was clearly a deeper drive to
express his animus against Alexander Hamilton and all his works—his
friends and allies, his system, his mind and political philosophy, his
ends and means.

In these diary notes—vivid, racy, almost prehensile in the way they
reach out for their target—Jefferson emerges as a political rhetorician of
no mean power, using a salty vocabulary of epithet. We see him on a
level considerably below the lofty plane of a disinterested public ser-
vant that formed his self-image. He seems too familiar with the wiles,
cabals, and maneuvers of his enemies to convince the reader that this is
alien territory to him. On the theory that it takes a conniver to catch a
conniver, one must be impressed with Jefferson's knowledge of the labyrinthine twists and turns in the corridors of power. His rhetoric of invec-
tive is a bit heavy-handed: "cabal and correspondence," "poison,"
"corrupt squadron," and "monarchy bottomed on corruption." But one
must remember that Jefferson was an eighteenth-century man, brought
up on the classical writers and the Whig-Tory struggles in England, and
carrying over into his party battles some of the same vocabulary—as
well as the same psychology—that he used against the British monarchy as a young revolutionary. His view of Hamilton as a "monarchy"
man served as a link between the new struggles and the earlier mood.

One gets from the *Anas* tantalizing glimpses of the little governing
circle of the new republic at work. The Cabinet was small—state, treasury, war, and attorney general—and while Henry Knox in the war post

was a mediocrity the others (Jefferson, Hamilton, Edmund Randolph) were the ablest to be found. Together with the president and with vice president Adams (who was not often consulted), they formed as talented a governing group as was to be found in any nation at the time. Jefferson's portraits do them something less than justice. While his portrait of Washington is majestically correct, that of Hamilton is at best grudging and at worst vicious, that of Randolph hostile, of Adams condescending, and of Knox contemptuous.

They sat in council over some issue repeatedly, and while Washington never left any doubt that the final judgment was his, he sought their opinions patiently, to a degree that became ever less true in later Cabinets. Everything was new, everything formed a first and set a precedent, and the crucial issues overlapped the departmental boundaries. By his very title—secretary of *state*—Jefferson was not meant to limit himself only to foreign affairs, and Hamilton could scarcely keep his hand out of them. There is a high drama in the way Jefferson describes the debates and the dissensions and decisions of the small governing elite in a new-born nation which was torn between the fears of an egalitarian leveling democracy and the fears of a limited monarchy-under-another-name.

Those fears were best symbolized and expressed by Jefferson and Hamilton. President Washington tried to mediate between the two young giants, thus engaged in the struggle for mastery, and get them to work in harness together. He never had a real chance of success. The struggle might have been moderated somewhat, and been slower and less fierce, if the British and French had not been engaged in a struggle of their own for the mastery of Europe and its colonial world. Willy-nilly the Americans were caught up in it. While it enabled them to strengthen their own independence by playing each of the Great Powers off against the other, and also heighten their national consciousness, the price they had to pay was a sharpened party consciousness within the nation that was getting its baptism of fire. Jefferson had to pay that price too, and the decade of the 1790s accordingly formed his decade of political embitterment as well as of political and personal growth in definiteness of outline.

Presidential Writings

The literary output of a president is necessarily limited. He is compelled to spend more time making history than writing it. But he does have inaugural speeches and annual State-of-the-Union messages to write and deliver, which offer him grand occasions to deploy his mind and style on an unparalleled stage. Jefferson's two Inaugurals have been equaled only by those of Lincoln, who was one of his greatest admirers and doubtless used Jefferson's as models.

Lincoln's First Inaugural, mainly a desperate plea to the southern states not to plunge the Union into a civil war, does not achieve the level of Jefferson's First in its serene confidence about the principles of a republican government. But Jefferson's Second Inaugural, earnestly giving an account of the gains made in the major problem-areas in four years, is matter-of-fact in comparison with the grand organ-tones of Lincoln's Second, with its awesome sense of the Civil War as God's punishment to both sides for the crime of slavery, and its compassionate plea for a wound-binding mood of charity between brothers who had killed brothers.

The danger with an address for an occasion is that one says either too little or too much in it, and that the solemnity of the occasion gives a stilted lameness to the language. Jefferson's First Inaugural escaped these dangers, partly because of Jefferson's skill with words to clothe his ideas in, but mainly because Jefferson knew how to bring all his life experience to bear on a great summing-up of principles—and that is what the First Inaugural is, just as the Declaration was a summing-up a quarter-century earlier.

The plea for unity ("We are all republicans: we are all federalists") was rather obviously strategic, especially in the light of Jefferson's later summary handling of some Federalists who had been all too Federalist. But there is nothing spurious about the other notes that Jefferson struck: that a democratic republic can allow its internal enemies ample scope for their opposition; that, being "the world's best hope," it does not suffer from the weakness that skeptics see in it, but is "the strongest government on earth"; that the great danger in America, parallel to the religious intolerance of Europe, is political intolerance and fanaticism; and that this can be resolved only through the principle of majority rule, which does not contradict the protection of the basic freedoms of religion, press, and the person, but is strengthened by them. The high point of the address comes at the end of the amazing long second paragraph which contains the heart of his political theory: "Sometimes it is said that man can not be trusted with the government of himself. Can he, then, be trusted with the government of others? Or have we found angels in the forms of kings to govern him? Let history answer this question."

This was Jefferson at his persuasive and felicitous best. It doesn't clinch that grand argument in defense of democracy to the elaboration of which Jefferson, in a sense, devoted his whole life. But his First Inaugural probably came closer than any other document in the language—closer than Lincoln's Gettysburg Address, and closer even than the Declaration of Independence—to outlining a defense by posing the crucial questions, even though Jefferson cannot answer them, but calls on history to do so. Where Lincoln's talk was elegiac, and the Declaration was magnificently and belligerently declarative, the Inaugural is probing and its mood—while confident—is reflective. It was a brilliant achievement. Instead of seeing it as only the prelude to the presidency itself, one might perversely—as an aficionado of theory rather than action—dare to see the first presidential term as an illustrative appendage of the speech.

In addition, Jefferson's addresses to the delegations of Indian chiefs who came to see him in Washington as president are among his most remarkable writings. Paternal in tone, as if he were talking to adolescents, they have a breathtaking simplicity of style which only underscores their basic dignity and keeps them almost invariably from the condescending. For Jefferson the Indian chiefs were more than the heads of minority groups. They were representatives of a state of Nature, natives of the American environment, but also evoking a sadness because of their failure to make full use of it. The addresses show the subtlety of Jefferson's mind, in his efforts to find the exactly right approaches to the Indian mentality. His aim was at once to persuade them to become farmers and artisans, and convert them to a new way of life, thus arresting the pathos of their decline in numbers and vigor, and at the same time to get them to cede and sell enough of their lands to the government so that the nation could extend its "empire for liberty." On both scores the addresses are masterpieces of rhetoric and persuasion. There is gentleness in them, but there is also a political sagacity, and a quiet pride of affirmation of American national interests.

Index

Tariffs, establishment of, 40, 43–44
Taylor, John, 43–44, 65
Tennis Court Oath, 33
Ternant, Jean-Baptiste, 46
Theocracies, intolerance of, 94
Theocritus, 109
Thomas Jefferson: A Life (Randall), 6
Thomas Jefferson: An Intimate History (Brodie), 4–5
Thomas Jefferson and His Times (Malone), 6
Thomas Jefferson and the Character Issue (article by Douglas Wilson), 6
Thucydides, 109
Thurmond, Strom, 124
Tobacco, 34
Tocqueville, Alexis de, 3, 23, 30, 77–78
Tripoli, pirates of, 76
Truman, Harry, 86, 128
Trumbull, John, 28
Turner, Frederick Jackson, 74
Tyler, John, 125

University of Virginia, founding of, 2, 93, 96, 99–103

Vergennes, Comte de, 34
Vice-president, Jefferson as, 64
Virgil, 109
Virginia Constitution, 18, 21

Virginia House of Burgesses, 17–18
Virginia Resolutions, 62
Voting rights, 18
Voyage Round the World in the Years 1740–1744 (Anson), 13

Walker, Betsy, 83
Walpole, Robert, 13
War of 1812, 97
Warren, Robert Penn, 124
Washington, George, 28, 32, 63, 120–121, 127, 139; presidential years of, 37–40, 64, 139
Watson, Tom, 128
Watt, James, 15, 25
Wealth of Nations, The (Smith), 25 n
Weights and measures, administration of, 38
Western territory: formation of new states in, 24; getting British out of, 47
West Indies, opening to American trade, 47
Whitney, Eli, 97
Wilkinson, General James, 79
William and Mary, College of, 13–14, 100
Williamsburg, 13–14
Wilson, Woodrow, 71
Wythe, George, 14–16, 29

XYZ episode, 53, 85